Published 2004 by Grange Books
an imprint of Grange Books PLC.
The Grange
Kings North Industrial Estate
Hoo nr. Rochester
Kent, UK
ME3 9ND
www.grangebooks.co.uk

All enquiries please email info@grangebooks.co.uk

Copyright ©2004 Taj Books Ltd

Copyright under International, Pan American, and Universal Copyright Conventions.
All rights reserved. No part of this book may be reproduced or transmitted in any form or by any means, electronic or mechanical, including photocopying, recording, or by any information storage-and-retrieval system, without written permission from the copyright holder.
Brief passages (not to exceed 1,000 words) may be qouted for reviews.

All notations of errors or omissions (author inquiries, permissions) concerning the content of this book should be addressed to:
TAJ Books 27, Ferndown Gardens, Cobham, Surrey, UK, KT11 2BH, info@tajbooks.com.

ISBN 1-84013-698-7

Printed in China.

1 2 3 4 5 08 07 06 05 04

MODERN WAR
DAY BY DAY

Alex Hook

1945 - 1949

World War II finishes **1945** | VE Day 8 May **1945** | VJ Day 8 August **1945** | Nuremberg trials **1946** | Greek Civil war **1946** | First Indo-Pakistan war **1947**

Having surrendered, Japanese soldiers march in formation past American occupation forces at Atsugi airfield at the end of the Second World War. Circa August 1945.

1945

August 1945
14 Japan surrenders

18 Russian forces overrun and take Manchuria.

22 China: Chinese civil war begins in earnest

September 1945
Korea: US forces arrive in South Korea in response to the Russian arrival in North Korea the month before. Partition is decided upon.

2 Japan: Gen Macarthur formally accepts Japanese surrender.

8 Victory over Japan Day.
Korea: US troops land at Inchon.

12 Indo-China: British troops under General Gracey land at Saigon.

23 Indo-China: Free French forces seize public buildings in Saigon and are disarmed by British.

October 1945
Indo-China: French colonial troops under General Leclerc replace British in Saigon.
Palestine: Beginning of the Jewish United Resistance Movement bombing campaign.

2 Vietnam: Cease-fire between Vietnamese and French troops.

17 Argentina: Colonel Juan Peron takes over as dictator.

November 1945
China: Nationalists launch an offensive in SW Manchuria, while the Communists consolidate their hold over Shentung province.

First Arab-Isreali war **1948** | Berlin blockade and airlift begins (continues until May 1949) **1948** | Mao Tse-tung proclaims Chinese People's Republic **1949** | End of Chinese Civil War **1949** | Malayan Emergency starts (ends 1966) **1949** | Creation of NATO **1949**

20 Nuremburg war crimes trials begin.

The accused in the dock, pictured at the IG Farben Trial of the Nuremberg Trials at the court in Nuremberg, Germany, 1947.

December 1945
21 Gen Patton dies in road accident.

1946

January 1946
France: General de Gaulle resigns.

27 China: Mao Ts-etung & Chiang Kai-shek agree to establish a National Army.

March 1946
Indo-China: Leclerc re-establishes French authority up to 16th parallel, and in Laos and Cambodia, Giau joins forces with Ho Chi Minh. The French negotiate a Chinese withdrawal from Tonkin.
Palestine: There is an Irgun attack on a British Army camp at Sarafand.

8 Germany: Nuremburg trial of Goering and Ribbentrop.

14 China: Truce between Chinese communists and nationalists agreed.

February 1946
India: Civil war looms as rioting erupts in Bombay.

2 Vietnam: Ho Chi Minh is elected President of the Communist Democratic Republic of Vietnam, which is recognised by France as a 'free state' within the French Union four days later.

7 Nuremburg trial of Hess

1945 - 1949

World War II finishes **1945** | VE Day 8 May **1945** | VJ Day 8 August **1945** | Nuremberg trials **1946** | Greek Civil war **1946** | First Indo-Pakistan war **1947**

Phase 3 of the Atom Bomb explosion in the Lagoon of Bikini Island.

13 Yugoslavia: Soldiers seize Tito's nationalist opponent, Gen Draja Mihailovich.

17 China: Nationalist checked at Szeping.

April 1946
Yugoslavia: The USA recognises Marshal Tito's People's Republic.
China: Nationalist offensive begins.
Palestine: Irgun attacks on railway.

25 Palestine: Jewish terrorists escalate their activities, killing seven people in a British Army car park.

28 China: Communists seize Tsitsihar, capital of Nunkiang province.

29 Japan: Tojo's trial begins.

May 1946
5 China: Civil war erupts between Communists & Nationalists on the Yangtse river.

22 China: Nationalists capture Changchun.

June 1946
China: Truce between Communist and Nationalist factions in the civil war.
India: Congress Party reject Britain's plan for an independent united India.
Palestine: Irgun men sentenced to death. British officers are then kidnapped in retaliation. Operation 'Agatha' launched.

July 1946
22 Palestine: Irgun bomb the offices of the Mandate in the King David Hotel, killing 91 people.

First Arab-Isreali war **1948**
Berlin blockade and airlift begins (continues until May 1949) **1948**
Mao Tse-tung proclaims Chinese People's Republic **1949**
End of Chinese Civil War **1949**
Malayan Emergency starts (ends 1966) **1949**
Creation of NATO **1949**

A view over the courtroom at the opening of the Nuremberg Trials, in the palace of justice in Nuremberg, Germany, 20 November 1945.

August 1946
India: Thousands die in rioting between Hindus and Muslims.
Palestine: Ships bringing Jewish refugees to Palestine are intercepted and turned back.
France: Fontainebleau Conference starts and continues till October without result.

September 1946
Greece: The Civil war begins again, Greek Nationalist troops fighting against Communist and Republican rebels.

October 1946
1 Greece: Fighting intensifies between Communists and Monarchists.

16 Germany: Top ten Nazis executed at Nuremburg

November 1946
Vietnam: The French occupy the Red River Delta against Viet Minh resistance. Ho Chi Minh and Giap withdraw to the mountains.

23 Vietnam: French shell the Viet Minh in Haipong.

December 1946
Palestine: Irgun kidnap British officers in retaliation for sentencing Irgun men to 'the cat'.

19 Vietnam: Viet Minh attack French troops in Hanoi. First Indo-Chinese War begins.

1947

January 1947
Palestine: Jewish rebels escalate further their

1945 - 1949

- World War II finishes **1945**
- VE Day 8 May **1945**
- VJ Day 8 August **1945**
- Nuremberg trials **1946**
- Greek Civil war **1946**
- First Indo-Pakistan war **1947**

A view over the craters of the southern peninsula of the island Helgoland in the Baltic Sea, northern Germany, 20 April 1947.

attacks on British targets. British garrison evacuates all non-essential personnel and families. Irgun and the Stern Gang, both Jewish terrorist groups, strike at military and police targets.

February 1947
India: Britain announces withdrawal by 1948.

March 1947
Palestine: Irgun and LHI attacks on British Army installations and personnel. Martial law is introduced. Irgun attack the Haifa oil refinery.

1 India: communal rioting and conflict between Hindus and Moslems.

19 China: Nationalists capture Yenan, the Communist capital.

April 1947
Palestine: Dov Gruner and three other Jewish terrorists are hanged.

May 1947
Palestine: Jewish terrorist break-out from Acre prison.

June 1947
1 India: Partition plans agreed between Hindus and Moslems.

July 1947
Palestine: LHI kidnap two British Army sergeants in retaliation for the death sentences imposed by military court—they later hang them.

1 Burma: Premier U Ang and six ministers assassinated.
Dutch East Indies: Dutch troops attack Indonesian Nationalists.

First Arab-Isreali war **1948**
Berlin blockade and airlift begins (continues until May 1949) **1948**
Mao Tse-tung proclaims Chinese People's Republic **1949**
End of Chinese Civil War **1949**
Malayan Emergency starts (ends 1966) **1949**
Creation of NATO **1949**

The first of some 600 German prisoners of war from Africa arrive at the Grunewald train station in Berlin, 24 June 1947.

18 Palestine: British ram the Jewish illegal immigrant ship *Exodus* on the high seas. They tow it to Haifa and repatriate the refugees to Germany.

August 1947
Palestine: UN General Assembly votes to establish partition.
Indo-China: French forces under General Valluy increased to 100,000. Bollaerts replaces d'Argenlieu as High Commissioner. Attempts are made to base a nationalist government on Emperor Bao Dai.

1 Dutch East Indies: UN broker truce.

15 India and Pakistan born, border clashes begin in Punjab.

September 1947
1 Palestine: UNSCOP issues its report, calling for the partition of Palestine.

October 1947
1 Syria: troops mass on their border with Palestine as the British leave.
The UN agrees to divide Palestine and set up a Jewish state, but the Arabs are furious and call for a crusade against the Jews.

15 India: Muslim tribesmen revolt in Kashmir.

26 India: In response to appeal from the Maharajah, Indian troops enter Kashmir to cement union of Kashmir with India and clash with rebels helped by Pakistani troops.

November 1947
29 Palestine: UN Partition Resolution—Palestine to be divided into separate Jewish and Arab states, with Jerusalem to be interna-

1945 - 1949

World War II finishes **1945** | VE Day 8 May **1945** | VJ Day 8 August **1945** | Nuremberg trials **1946** | Greek Civil war **1946** | First Indo-Pakistan war **1947**

It was ironic that Gandhi, the exponent of peaceful protest, should be assassinated by direct action.

tionalised. The Arab countries and Arab league refuse to recognise this resolution.

December 1947
1 Palestine: Arabs riot in Jerusalem, which they then blockade. Skirmishes, road ambushes, riots, bombings and massacres start—instigated by both Jews and Arabs.

1948

January 1948
Palestine: Arab Salvation Army (aka Arab Liberation Army—ALA) is admitted into Palestine by the British, following a promise not to attack Jews. Circumventing the UN and US arms embargoes, the Jewish Agency concludes an arms deal with Czechoslovakia: most of the equipment arrives in June, after the British have left. Arab countries, as independent states, purchase arms legally on the open market.

1 Slovakia: Communists seize power.

3 Pakistan: Pakistan accuses India of armed aggression.

30 India: Gandhi assassinated by Nathuram Godse.

February 1948
8 Korea: The North Korean People's Army (NKA) is officially activated.

March 1948
India: Pakistani inspired attack on Poonch. India counter-attacks in Kashmir.

April 1948
Palestine: Fighting between Jews and Arabs.
Indo-China: The French agree to provisional

First Arab-Isreali war **1948**
Berlin blockade and airlift begins (continues until May 1949) **1948**
Mao Tse-tung proclaims Chinese People's Republic **1949**
End of Chinese Civil War **1949**
Malayan Emergency starts (ends 1966) **1949**
Creation of NATO **1949**

A view of the destroyed east wing of the city hall in Frankfurt, western Germany, 1948.

government of Vietnam under Bao Dai.
India: The UN Security Council calls on India and Pakistan to withdraw from Kashmir.

1 Berlin: USSR begins ground blockade.

6 Palestine: the Arab blockade of Jerusalem is broken temporarily by Operation 'Nachshon'. Death of the foremost Palestinian military leader Abd-El-Qader Al-Husseini, shot by a Jewish sentry when he enters Jewish held Kastel, thinking it is in Arab hands.

9 Palestine: The Deir Yassin Massacre—Jewish dissident underground groups—Irgun and Lehi kill over 100 Palestinian civilians in the Jerusalem village of Deir Yassin.

13 Palestine: The Haddassah Convoy Massacre—In retaliation for Deir Yassin, Arabs kill Jewish medical personnel and casualties as they travel to Hadassah hospital.

Operation 'Har'el', launched by Hagannah at conclusion of Operation 'Nachshon', —which does not succeed in opening the road to Jerusalem.

22 Palestine: Operation 'Misparayim' is launched by Hagannah, its aim to assume control of Haifa after the British.

28 Costa Rica: Rebels enter the capital after weeks of civil war.

May 1948

India: Indians capture Tithwal and face Pakistani troops, who reinforce Kashmir.

1 Slovakia: Communists seize power.

12 Palestine: Haganah captures Tsfat.

1945 - 1949

- World War II finishes **1945**
- VE Day 8 May **1945**
- VJ Day 8 August **1945**
- Nuremberg trials **1946**
- Greek Civil war **1946**
- First Indo-Pakistan war **1947**

13 Palestine: Jaffa surrenders to Haganah.

14 Israel: The State of Israel born, and immediately invaded by Arab neighbours. The Arab Israeli war begins. Gush Etzion Massacre—In retaliation for Deir Yassin Massacre, Arabs killed over 50 Jewish defenders at Gush Etzion, after they had surrendered.

17 Israel: Haganah captures Acco (Acre).

18 Israel: Syrian army captures Massada and Merom Hagolan.

28 Israel: The Jewish quarter of Jerusalem falls to the Jordan Legion. About 300 Haganah defenders are taken prisoner. The entire quarter, including 58 of 59 synagogues, is demolished by an Arab mob despite efforts of the Legion.

29 Palestine: UN Security Council resolution for a truce.

The industrial magnate Alfried Krupp von Bohlen und Halbach, former sole owner of the Krupp company since 1943, holds his closing statement at the Nuremberg Trials at the court in Nuremberg.

June 1948

Palestine: First UN cease-fire. Attempt of *Altalena* to land arms.

1 Malaya: Rubbers planters attacked by Communist rebels.

16 Malaya: State of Emergency declared, Sir Edward Gent, British High Commissioner, is dismissed.

23 Palestine: Irgun's *Altalena* ship brings weapons—a violation of UN embargo. However the Israeli government agrees to it, provided that Irgun hands over the weapons to IDF and forms a unified force. Irgun refuses. Palmach units of IDF then take the weapons by force, killing 14 Irgun men.

First Arab-Isreali war **1948** | Berlin blockade and airlift begins (continues until May 1949) **1948** | Mao Tse-tung proclaims Chinese People's Republic **1949** | End of Chinese Civil War **1949** | Malayan Emergency starts (ends 1966) **1949** | Creation of NATO **1949**

Feild Marshall Viscount Montgomery of Alamein, one of the British Army Commanders of the Second World War.

28 Malaya: Sir Edward Gent, High Commissioner killed in air crash.

July 1948

Palestine: Israeli attacks on Lydda, Ramleh and Latrun; also the breaking of the Arab siege of Jerusalem. The Egyptian army then attacks from Majdal and an Israeli counterattack at Faluja proves unsuccessful. Israel also bombs Cairo, Damascus and Rafa using its first (old WW2) aircraft. Second UN cease-fire.
Malaya: Major-General Boucher produces British Army plan.
India: Pakistan attacks in Ladakh.

12 Palestine: The Egyptians attack Kibbutz Negba and are rebuffed with heavy casualties.

August 1948

12 Germany: Soviet troops open fire on Germans protesting against occupation of Berlin.

September 1948

Palestine: The second UN cease-fire ends. Irgun and LHI disbanded.
India: India occupies Hyderabad.
Korea: Kim Il-sung proclaims Peoples' Democratic Republic of Korea with himself as President.

17 Palestine: Swedish Count Folke Bernadotte, a UN mediator, assassinated in Jerusalem.

22 Palestine: The establishment of the Government of All Palestine—sponsored by Egypt and the Arab League. Its flag that of the 1916 Arab Revolt, with Jerusalem to be the capital and Gaza the seat of government.

1945 - 1949

World War II finishes **1945** | VE Day 8 May **1945** | VJ Day 8 August **1945** | Nuremberg trials **1946** | Greek Civil war **1946** | First Indo-Pakistan war **1947**

The military governors of the three western occupation zones,.

October 1948
Palestine: Israeli attacks result in occupation of Negev and eviction of Lebanese and Syrian forces from Galilee. Third UN cease-fire starts.

15 Palestine: Third truce ends; Israeli offensive breaks Egyptian siege of settlements in the Negev. In the north, Operation 'Hiram' defeats the ALA. IDF massacres in Arab villages.

30 China: Mukden captured by Communists, Nationalists retreat.

December 1948
Palestine: Israeli attacks at Falluja and Gaza.
Korea: Russian occupation troops leave.

11 Palestine: UN Resolution 194 calls for cessation of hostilities. Beginning of Israeli Operation 'Horev' which captures Gaza and enters Sinai. Pressure from Britain and USA will lead to Israeli withdrawal.

1949

January 1949
India: Pakistan accuses India of armed aggression. Cease-fire in Kashmir, supervised by UN.

1 China: Peking taken by Communists.
India: UN broker truce between Indian and Pakistani—almost all Kashmir is now in Indian hands.

2 Dutch East Indies: Java under Dutch army control.

3 S Africa: Hundreds die in race riots.

4 Burma: Independence declared.

February 1949
Palestine: Israel and Arab states agree to an armistice in separate agreements. Gaza falls

- First Arab-Isreali war **1948**
- Berlin blockade and airlift begins (continues until May 1949) **1948**
- Mao Tse-tung proclaims Chinese People's Republic **1949**
- End of Chinese Civil War **1949**
- Malayan Emergency starts (ends 1966) **1949**
- Creation of NATO **1949**

General view of the official signing ceremony creating the North Atlantic Treaty Organization (NATO) in Washington.

under the jurisdiction of Egypt. The West Bank of the Jordan is annexed by Israel.

24 Middle East: In Rhodes an armistice is signed between Egypt and Israel, but many contentious issues are left unresolved and the State of Israel is not recognised by the Arabs.

March 1949

Greece: Communist rebels begin offensives in Macedonia and Thrace.

7 Palestine: Operation 'Uvda'—IDF captures southern Negev, including Eilat.

11 Middle East: Jordan and Israel sign a cease-fire.

April 1949

Costa Rica: Rebels led by Colonel Jose Figueres enter the capital after some weeks of civil war.

Palestine: Israel signs armistice with Jordan.

4 USA: Twelve nations sign in the creation of the North Atlantic Treaty Organisation (NATO) treaty in Washington.

26 Indonesia: South Molucca declares its independence from Sukarno's Indonesia.

May 1949

Czechoslovakia: Communists seize power throughout Czechoslovakia.
The Western Allies (USA, Great Britain and France) set up a Military Security Board for West Germany in early February and the Federal Republic of (West) Germany is \founded.
Palestine: UN recognizes Israel and Jordan as independent states.

1945 - 1949

World War II finishes **1945** | VE Day 8 May **1945** | VJ Day 8 August **1945** | Nuremberg trials **1946** | Greek Civil war **1946** | First Indo-Pakistan war **1947**

King George VI (c) accompanied by Group Captain B.C. Yarde inspects the Berlin air-lift personnel at the parade in London.

Indo-China: French National Assembly approves union of Vietnam, Laos and Cambodia. General Revers reviews situation.

12 Germany: Soviet blockade of Berlin ends.

26 China: Shanghai falls to the Communists, Nationalists withdraw to Canton.

June 1949
Korea: The last US combat troops leave.

11 Middle East: Another UN brokered truce begins.

July 1949
Malaya: General Harding succeeds General Ritchie as British Army C-in-C Far East. The Communist Party is banned and British troops wipe out a network of hideouts in the Kuala Lumpur area. Hong Kong: British garrison considerably increased.

9 Middle East: Heavy fighting breaks out for a further ten days between Arabs and Jews.

August 1949
Greece: Greek communist rebels (Elas) defeated in the Vitsi mountains.

28 USSR: Soviets send troops to the border to threaten Tito's Yugoslavia.

September 1949
India: Hyderabad surrenders, overwhelmed by Indian Army troops.
Middle East: Egypt sues for peace.

9 Korea: North Korea formally declares its independence, but commits itself to reuniting the Peninsula—by force of arms if necessary.

First Arab-Isreali war **1948** | Berlin blockade and airlift begins (continues until May 1949) **1948** | Mao Tse-tung proclaims Chinese People's Republic **1949** | End of Chinese Civil War **1949** | Malayan Emergency starts (ends 1966) **1949** | Creation of NATO **1949**

October 1949
China: Canton falls to the Communists.
Germany: The German Democratic Republic (DDR/East Germany) comes into existence.
Indo-China: Mao Tse-tung establishes authority over China; proclaims People's Republic.

16 Greece: Elas communist rebels stop fighting.

30 China: Mukden is captured by the Communists, completing their take-over of Manchuria. The Nationalist armies are retreating southwards and, despite massive US aid, are clearly being beaten by the Communists.

November 1949
Middle East: In further talks the Egyptians demand control of the Negev, while Israel demands their withdrawal from the Gaza Strip.
Malaya: British launch a drive against the communist rebels.
21 China: Mao proclaims People's Republic of

Mao Tse Tung, the Chairman of the Communist Party of China and leader of the People's Republic of China.

China in Peking.

December 1949
Chiang Kai-shek acknowledges defeat and resigns from the presidency of the Nationalist Government.

8 China: Nationalist regime moves to the Island of Taiwan

1950

January 1950
Indo-China: Ho Chi Minh claims his is the only representative government of Vietnam; recognized by China and Russia. The USA recognises government of Bao Dai and grants military aid.
Korea: US Secretary of State, Dean Acheson,

1950-1959

- Korean War starts on 25 June **1950**
- Chinese invade Tibet **1950**
- Indo-Chinese (Vietnam) War starts **1951**
- Korean war ends 26 July **1953**
- Mau Mau Emergency in Kenya starts (ends 1955) **1953**
- Cyprus Emergency starts (ends 1962) **1954**

The South Korean on the left is guarding two North Koreans captured on a northern sector of the front and brought to a forward command post.

defines US defence commitment in Pacific.

February 1950
Vietnam: Western powers formally recognise Bao Dai's French-supported regime, while the USSR recognises Ho Chi Minh's government, effectively splitting Vietnam into two. Meanwhile Giap starts attacks on isolated French garrisons, now under command of General Carpentier.

15 China: China and the USSR sign a friendship pact. The Soviets agree to give up war booty taken in Manchuria, also to give up the Manchurian railway and Port Arthur by 1952.

March 1950
Malaya: An additional Gurkha brigade is deployed from Hong Kong.

April 1950
Malaya: Lt-Gen Sir Harold Briggs appointed as Director of Operations; produces the Briggs Plan.

May 1950
Malaya: Chin Peng's MRLA'S attacks now running at average of 400 a month. Operations under Briggs Plan start.

June 1950
Malaya: Lt-Gen Briggs sets up a Federal War Council which plans compulsory resettlement in new villages for Chinese squatters.
Cyprus: Michael Mouskos elected Archbishop Makarios III and Ethnarch.

18 Egypt: Egypt signs a security pact with Lebanon, Saudi Arabia, Syria and Yemen.

25 Korea: The North Korean Army (NKA) with seven divisions and 150 T34 tanks invades the Republic of South Korea (ROK) warning.

Algerian Emergency starts **1954** Warsaw Pact created 14 May **1955** Suez Crisis: Second Arab-Israeli War **1956** Hungarian uprising 23 October **1956** Aden Emergency starts (ends 1967) **1958** Fidel Castro deposes Batista regime in Cuba **1959**

Contingent of British Troops for the United Nations get Ready to set Sail from Southampton.

USA: UN Security Council demands NK stop its attack and return to its borders

28 Korea: B-26 aircraft shot down at Han.

29 Korea: the ROK Capitol Seoul falls, and bridges across Han River are destroyed, leaving most of the ROK army trapped on northern shore.

30 Korea: NKA 3rd Division crosses Han River. President Truman commits US troops to enforce UN demand.

July 1950
Malaya: 3 Commando Brigade Royal Marines deployed from Hong Kong.
Korea: US forces increased to 47,000. Eighth Army deployed with General Walker OC.

3 Korea: ROK forces mistakenly attacked by US and Australian air units.

5 Korea: US Task Force Smith crushed by NKA 4th Division.

7 Korea: United Nations Command created, under General Douglas MacArthur

8 Korea: US defeated at Chonan.

10 Korea: US air attacks on NKA cover US troops retreating along the Seoul-Taejon road.

12–23 Korea: Taejon falls, as two NKA divisions smash up US 24th Infantry Division, capturing most of their equipment and taking prisoner the commanding officer, Maj-Gen Dean.
13 Korea: Lt-Gen Walton Walker takes command of ground forces in Korea. The US and

1950-1959

Korean War starts on 25 June **1950**
Chinese invade Tibet **1950**
Indo-Chinese (Vietnam) War starts **1951**
Korean war ends 26 July **1953**
Mau Mau Emergency in Kenya starts (ends 1955) **1953**
Cyprus Emergency starts (ends 1962) **1954**

Field Marshal Alexander, British Defence Minister, in Korea. (L-R): General Van Fleet; the Field Marshal; and Brigadier General Bostner in Compound 76.

ROK forces form line from Kum river through Chongju to the coast at Pyonghae-ri. The NKA begin a general assault along the Kum river.

24 Korea: NKA captures Yongdong—but halts its attack after taking over 2,000 casualties—mostly from artillery bombarments. Next assaults down the west coast, outflanking the Eighth Army which withdraws to prepared positions. Another NKA division threatens to take Pusan and cut off all US/UN forces in Korea.

28 Korea: NKA captures Chinju.

29 Korea: General Walker issues 'Stand or Die' order.

August 1950

1 Korea: US and ROK troops fall further back, but establish a 'Pusan Perimeter' defence line along the Naktong river.

7 Korea: 25th Infantry Division makes first US counter attack—unsuccessful.

13 Korea: First Battle of the Naktong Bulge. NKA assault across the Naktong against US 24th Division and ROK—and almost break through. The US Marine Brigade is brought into action closely supported by carrier-based Corsair Squadrons and manage to throw NKA back across the Naktong, in the process virtually eliminating them as a fighting force.

17 Korea: Massacre of prisoners at Hill 303.
18 Korea: In savage fighting ROK stops NKA at Pusan.

Algerian Emergency starts **1954** · Warsaw Pact created 14 May **1955** · Suez Crisis; Second Arab-Israeli War **1956** · Hungarian uprising 23 October **1956** · Aden Emergency starts (ends 1967) **1958** · Fidel Castro deposes Batista regime in Cuba **1959**

29 Korea: British Commonwealth 27th Brigade lands at Pusan.

September 1950
1 Korea: NKA launches five simultaneous assaults along the Naktong.

3 Korea: US attacks around Yongsan.

15 Korea: Continuous and savage fighting around the Pusan Perimeter.

17 Korea: In a bold move MacArthur lands two divisions at Inchon and links up with Eighth Army advancing from Pusan.

19 Korea: Yongdungpo and embattled Seoul are recaptured by US/UN forces.

27 Korea: MacArthur given permission to cross the 38th Parallel into North Korea, but forbidden to cross the Yalu river.

A United States soldier in a Jeep bound for the front line in Korea watches as an elderly Korean refugee flees the advancing North Korean troops. The old man has all his worldly goods on his back as he trudges along, seeking safety.

30 Korea: ROK troops cross 38th Parallel.

October 1950
Indo-China: Giap's attacks force French to abandon most of Red River Delta.

9 Korea: 1st Cavalry Division leads UN-sanctioned general assault across 38th Parallel to reunify all of Korea.

14 Korea: Lead Elements of CCF 38th Field Army cross the Yalu at Andong to begin China's support of North Korea
19 Korea: NK capitol Pyongyang falls, followed by mass North Korean surrenders.

20 Korea: MacArthur meets Truman. US/UN

1950-1959

- Korean War starts on 25 June **1950**
- Chinese invade Tibet **1950**
- Indo-Chinese (Vietnam) War starts **1951**
- Korean war ends 26 July **1953**
- Mau Mau Emergency in Kenya starts (ends 1955) **1953**
- Cyprus Emergency starts (ends 1962) **1954**

Pte. John Oates of Halifax and Pte. Alex Rolland, both of the Argyll and Sutherland Highlanders manning a Bren gun as they keep watch for Chinese Communist troops at the front in Korea.

airborne assault north of Pyongyang

21 Tibet: Chinese troops invade, reaching Lhasa by the 30th.

25 Korea: ROK 6th Division become the first UN troops to meet and get beaten by CCF 42nd Field Army around Chosan.

26 Korea: 1st Marine Division and X Corps land on east coast at Wonsan

31 Vietnam: Following Viet Minh victories at Dong Khe, Cao Bang, Lang Son and That Khe the French have to give up the region adjoining the Chinese border by the end of the year.

November 1950

Korea: In the first week of the month the CCF opens China's First Phase offensive, by defeating 1st Cav and the ROK, driving UN forces back to the Chongchon river. In the east the only UN success is the 7th Marine Regiment destroying the CCF 124th Division

Indo-China: Marshal Juin's visit leads to replacement of Carpentier and Pignon by Marshal de Lattre as High Commisioner and C-in-C.

4 Korea: MacArthur intensifies bombing of communications routes to and from the Yalu.

8 Korea: A MiG-15 is shot down in the first all-jet dogfight.

21 Korea: US 17th Regiment reaches the Yalu.

25 Korea: UN offensive begins from the Chongchon river.

Algerian Emergency starts **1954** | Warsaw Pact created 14 May **1955** | Suez Crisis: Second Arab-Israeli War **1956** | Hungarian uprising 23 October **1956** | Aden Emergency starts (ends 1967) **1958** | Fidel Castro deposes Batista regime in Cuba **1959**

These cheerful Royal Air Force pilots typify the joint efforts of the United Nations in Korea, where they are flying with an F-86 Sabrejet unit of the united States Air Force.

26 Korea: Over the next four days US 2nd and 25th Divisions are defeated and Eighth Army begins general retreat in the west

27 Korea: Four CCF Armies attack 1st Marine Div and 7th Infantry Div at Chosin Reservoir.

30 Korea: President Truman threatens use of atomic weapons against CCF.

December 1950

Tibet: The Dalai Lama flees the country.

11 Korea: 1st Marine Division fights through encircling CCF forces to reach US/UN lines. The 10 CCF divisions attacking in Chosin are badly mauled. UN Naval forces begin evacuation at Hungnam
14 Korea: UN passes a Cease Fire resolution

19 USA: General Eisenhower is appointed supreme commander of NATO.

23 Korea: General Walker killed in accident and succeeded by Ridgway.
24 Korea: Last of X Corps evacuated from Hungnam.

1951

January 1951

Korea: Arguments oscillate between MacArthur and Washington over future strategy of the war.

1 Korea: Chinese and N Koreans launch an allout attack over the 38th Parallel.

4 Korea: Seoul falls again to NKA.

13 Vietnam: General Giap begins a new drive on Hanoi, but the Viet Minh are repulsed by

1950-1959

- Korean War starts on 25 June **1950**
- Chinese invade Tibet **1950**
- Indo-Chinese (Vietnam) War starts **1951**
- Korean war ends 26 July **1953**
- Mau Mau Emergency in Kenya starts (ends 1955) **1953**
- Cyprus Emergency starts (ends 1962) **1954**

Carrying rifles with needle-pointed bayonets and clad in their winter quilted uniforms, Chinese military police volunteers with the North Korean forces gaze towards the tents, scene of the weeks-long ceasefire talks.

the French at Vinh Yen.

14 Korea: UN forces counterattack and retake the capital. Ridgway stabilises UN lines along the 37th parallel.

24 Korea: Ridgway launches Operation 'Thunderbolt' counter-offensive to Han River.

February 1951
1 Korea: UN resolution to end the Korean War.

11 Korea: CCF counterattacks at Hoengsong, destroys ROK 8th Div.

14 Korea: UN forces stop CCF at Chipyong-ni.

March 1951
Korea: Operation 'Ripper'—the US Eighth Army re-crosses the Han. Chunchon recaptured and the Idaho Line reached against a weak opposition, as CCF regroups.
Vietnam: A second Communist assault on Mao Khe is also defeated.

7 Iran: Prime Minister Ali Razmara is assassinated and in April is replaced by Mossadegh.

15 Iran: martial law is proclaimed, with troops and tanks on the streets of Tehran.

17 Korea: Gen Ridgway's Operation 'Killer' has limited success clearing CCF from Chipyong-ni and the mountains to the east.
20 UK: Field Marshal Montgomery is appointed General Eisenhower's deputy at SHAPE.

April 1951
Korea: Operations 'Rugged' and 'Dauntless'

Algerian Emergency starts **1954** • Warsaw Pact created 14 May **1955** • Suez Crisis; Second Arab-Israeli War **1956** • Hungarian uprising 23 October **1956** • Aden Emergency starts (ends 1967) **1958** • Fidel Castro deposes Batista regime in Cuba **1959**

United States infantry move to the front line as civilians, caught in the fighting between United Nations forces and North Korean invaders, evacuate their homes and move to a place of safety. One of the women carries her baby on her back.

drive 15 miles north of Kansas Line.

8 Korea: All N Korean and Chinese forces have withdrawn from S Korea and the front is stabilised on the 38th Parallel. General MacArthur advocates the invasion of China and the use of A-bombs.

11 Korea: MacArthur dismissed by Truman, his place is taken by General Ridgway.

15 Korea: General James Van Fleet assumes command of Eighth Army.

22 Korea: The Chinese and N Koreans attack again, but after initial successes they are held roughly along the line of the Imjin River. After further heavy fighting the front stabilises.

24 Korea: A heavily outnumbered US/UN force stops CCF at Kapyong Valley.

30 Korea: CCF and NKA pull back to regroup.

May 1951

Korea: Major fighting in area of 38th parallel.
Indo-China: Battle of Phat Diem.
Malaya: General Keightley succeeds General Harding as C-in-C British Army Far East.

5 Korea: Second CCF spring offensive begins.
20 Korea: CCF offensive stopped after penetrating 30 miles into the east-central region

23 Tibet: Chinese and Tibetans sign a peace treaty, but guerrilla warfare continues.

1950-1959

- **Korean War starts on 25 June 1950**
- **Chinese invade Tibet 1950**
- **Indo-Chinese (Vietnam) War starts 1951**
- **Korean war ends 26 July 1953**
- **Mau Mau Emergency in Kenya starts (ends 1955) 1953**
- **Cyprus Emergency starts (ends 1962) 1954**

The 1st Battalion, Royal Warwickshire Regiment, on board their troopship at Southampton, bound for Korea. Nearly 70% of the men are National Servicemen.

June 1951

Korea: First Meeting of Armistice Commission at Kaesong. Fighting continues on 38th parallel.
Cyprus: Grivas arrives and prepares plan of campaign.
Vietnam: Third assault on the Day River line south of Hanoi is again defeated.
Malaya: Troubles continue with terrorist threats stopping work in many plantations. In response Operation 'Starvation' is put into effect by the British.

1 Korea: UN resumes attack northwards, regains both Line Kansas and the Wyoming bulge by mid-June. CCF 180th Division totally destroyed.
10 Korea: beginning of a week's fighting in the Punchbowl, near the Hwachon Reservoir. 1st Marine Division reaches the northern ridges pushing back the NKA in some brutal fighting.

13 Korea: Fighting now lapses down to smaller scale individual unit skirmishes.

July 1951

Korea: Washington orders Van Fleet to halt his attack and wait for armistice negotiations. UN forms a Main Line of Resistance (MLR) The Communists use this pause to recoup their heavy losses, and build up positions opposite the MLR.
Jordan: Assassination of Jordan's King Abdulla because of rumoured plans for peace with Israel. His grandson Hussein crowned in his place following the brief reign of Tallal.
10 Korea: Truce talks begin at Kaesong.

August 1951

4 Korea: Communists break off talks.

17 Korea: Beginning of the Battle of Bloody Ridge.

Algerian Emergency starts **1954**	Warsaw Pact created 14 May **1955**	Suez Crisis: Second Arab-Israeli War **1956**	Hungarian uprising 23 October **1956**	Aden Emergency starts (ends 1967) **1958**	Fidel Castro deposes Batista regime in Cuba **1959**

September 1951

India: China suggests discussions to stabilise the frontiers of Tibet.

5 Korea: Beginning of the Battle for Heartbreak Ridge

6 Korea: Battle of Bloody Ridge ends.

8 Japan: 48 nations sign a peace treaty with Japan.

9 Tibet: The Chinese occupy Lhasa.

23 Korea: End of Heartbreak Ridge battle.

October 1951
Indo-China: Battle of Nglia Lo.
Korea: Operation 'Commando' lasts till 23rd. Five UN divisions attack elements of four CCF armies. In the savage fighting, the CCF suffer over 21,000 casualties, the UN around 4,000.

Hands behind heads, sullen North Korean prisoners kneel as they wait, under armed guard, for questioning after they had been captured by American forces 'somewhere in Korea'.

6 Malaya: Sir Henry Gurney, the High Commissioner, is killed in an ambush by the MRPLA near Kuala Lumpur.

8 Egypt: Egypt renounces the Anglo-Egyptian treaty, British troops take control of the Suez Canal a few days later and frequent clashes take place thereafter. From mid-November British civilians are evacuated.

25 Korea: Peace talks resume at Kaesong

November 1951
14 Vietnam: French paratroops recapture Hao Binh under De Lattre —who then returns to France; succeeded by General Salan.

27 Korea: Truce talks continue at Panmunjom

1950–1959

- **1950** Korean War starts on 25 June
- **1950** Chinese invade Tibet
- **1951** Indo-Chinese (Vietnam) War starts
- **1953** Korean war ends 26 July
- **1953** Mau Mau Emergency in Kenya starts (ends 1955)
- **1954** Cyprus Emergency starts (ends 1962)

Members of two of the forces fighting under the United Nations flag in South Korea meet for a cigarette. (l) Cpl. Tony Gibbs of the 1st Middlesex Regiment (British Army) and Pte. Peter Merchain of the United States 8th Army..

December 1951
Malaya: Briggs retires; replaced by General Sir Rob Lockhart. Police Commissioner Gray replaced by Sir Arthur Young.
Indo-China: Giap counterattacks Hoa Binh. Salan orders withdrawal.

18 Korea: Exchange of POW lists.

1952

January 1952
Bolivia: Revolution overthrows the military government of General Ballivan.
Malaya: Alliance Party formed.

2 Korea: UN POW Exchange Proposal proposed. It is rejected by Communists the next day.

25 Egypt: British troops seize the Ismailia police station.

February 1952
Malaya: General Templar is appointed high commissioner and director of operations. He takes the fight to the insurgents, and tries to win 'hearts and minds' of the people.

18 Korea: Riots in Koje-do prison camp.

March 1952
2 Egypt: Parliament is suspended.
13 Korea: More rioting in Koje-do prison camp.

April 1952
25 Vietnam: French troops launch an attack on a Viet Minh base at Tay Ninh.

- Algerian Emergency starts **1954**
- Warsaw Pact created 14 May **1955**
- Suez Crisis; Second Arab-Israeli War **1956**
- Hungarian uprising 23 October **1956**
- Aden Emergency starts (ends 1967) **1958**
- Fidel Castro deposes Batista regime in Cuba **1959**

An American tank stands guard as a lorry full of British troops moves toward a frontline in South Korea. The troops belong to the 1st Middlesex Regiment.

May 1952

7 Korea: Gen Dodd captured by Koje-do POWs.

22 Egypt: A military coup is launched, led by Colonel Nasser and General Neguib, is then followed by widespread rioting in Cairo.

27 Korea: Syngman Rhee declares martial law at Pusan.

30 Korea: General Mark Clark takes over UN command. Fighting is now static, but fierce.

June 1952

S Africa: The African National Congress organises demonstrations against apartheid.
Korea: June—Oct Vicious, bitter localized fighting along MLR as truce talks drag on.

12 Korea: General Haydon Boatner replaces General Colson at Koje-do and ends the rioting. General Mark Clark assumes FECOM from General Ridgway.

23 Korea: General Clark orders the bombing of NK power plants.

July 1952

23 Korea: US air strikes knock out North Korea's hydroelectric power stations close to Pyongyang for over two weeks.

26 Egypt: King Faruq is forced to abdicate and exiled.

27 Egypt: New governing authority, the Revolutionary Command Council, is established and chaired by Nasser.

1950-1959

- Korean War starts on 25 June **1950**
- Chinese invade Tibet **1950**
- Indo-Chinese (Vietnam) War starts **1951**
- Korean war ends 26 July **1953**
- Mau Mau Emergency in Kenya starts (ends 1955) **1953**
- Cyprus Emergency starts (ends 1962) **1954**

(Above) An American casualty is carried on a stretcher from an ambulance plane at an airport in Japan.
(Left) Servicemane with high spirits aboard the 'Empire Orwell' as it leaves for Hong Kong from Southampton.

August 1952

12–25 Korea: US Marines capture Hill 122 east of Panmunjom, and hold it against repeated attacks.

29 Korea: Largest air strike of the war—1,400 aircraft hit the North Korean capital, Pyongyang.

September 1952

17–24 Korea: Outpost Kelly battle.

October 1952

6–15 Korea: Battle of White Horse Hill—ROK 9th Division inflicts 10,000 casualties on CCF while repelling repeated assaults, helped largely by information from Chinese deserters.

8–18 November Korea: Truce talks halted. General Clark initiates Operation 'Showdown'.

9 Kenya: Chief Warukiu murdered.

15 Vietnam: Viet Minh forces mount a major offensive in the Thai highlands. Giap renews offensive at Nglia Lo. Salan counterattacks in Clear River valley.

20 Kenya: Mau Mau Emergency. The British authorities declare a state of emergency as British troops arrive. Some 2,000 Kikuyu including Jorno Kenyatta are arrested.

26–28 Korea: 1st Battalion of the Black Watch and Commonwealth Division tanks fight off the CCF in the Battle of The Hook.

November 1952

Vietnam: Salan withdraws to de Lattre line and concentrates on clearing Annam and Mekong Delta.

3 Korea: Battle for Heartbreak Ridge 2.

Algerian Emergency starts **1954** | Warsaw Pact created 14 May **1955** | Suez Crisis: Second Arab-Israeli War **1956** | Hungarian uprising 23 October **1956** | Aden Emergency starts (ends 1967) **1958** | Fidel Castro deposes Batista regime in Cuba **1959**

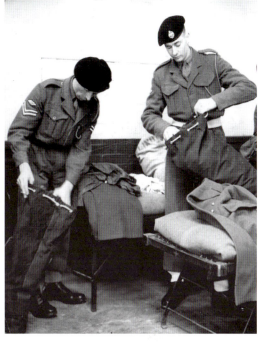

(Above) Men of the 1st Royal Tank Regiment pack their kit in readiness for their departure for Korea.
(Left) A joyful reunion at Southampton docks.

December 1952

25 Korea: UN beats off a savage CCF assault at T-Bone Hill.
26 Korea: The stalemate continues—as do deadly small-unit battles, President-Elect Eisenhower visits.

1953

January 1953

Kenya: Ruck family murdered. Settlers march on Government House.

25 Korea: US/UN launch Operation 'Smack', which becomes the battle of Spud Hill, against an enemy strongpoint on T-Bone. In spite of heavy tank and air support the attack is repulsed with heavy casualties.

February 1953

Kenya: Lari massacre.

11 Korea: General Maxwell Taylor takes command of US Eigth Army.

March 1953

5 USSR: Stalin dies. The new USSR Premie is, Georgi Malenkov.

28 Korea: NK Premier Kim Il Sung and CCF Peng Teh-huai agree to the exchange of POWs.

30 Korea: Truce talks resume at Panmunjom.

April 1953

Kenya: Hinde becomes Director of Operations. 39th British Infantry Brigade deployed.
Korea: More savage fighting around Old Baldy, T-bone, outpost Eerie and Pork Chop, with these features regularly changing hands.

1950-1959

- Korean War starts on 25 June **1950**
- Chinese invade Tibet **1950**
- Indo-Chinese (Vietnam) War starts **1951**
- Korean war ends 26 July **1953**
- Mau Mau Emergency in Kenya starts (ends 1955) **1953**
- Cyprus Emergency starts (ends 1962) **1954**

Private Adam Maxwell (left) holds his cup as Segeant Major Robert Murray serves the tea. They are shown here at a British Forces field kitchen in Korea.

10 Laos: The Viet Minh invade and by December have reached the River Mekong along the Thai border.

17–18 Korea: Parts of Little Gibraltar feature lost and retaken and US/UN infantry suffer heavy casualties at Pork Chop Hill.

20 Korea: Exchange of sick and wounded POWs.

23 Korea: Panmunjom talks resume yet again…

May 1953
Indo-China: General Navarre succeeds Salan; plans period of consolidation and development of Vietnam National Army.
Korea: Exchange of prisoners starts. The Chinese launch a surprise last-ditch offensive.

June 1953
Colombia: General Pinilla leads a coup.

Kenya: General Sir George Erskine arrives as C-in-C.

6 Korea: US 7th Infantry Division suffer heavy casualties at Pork Chop Hill, so are withdrawn.

14 Korea: NKA/CCF attack drives back ROK positions.

16 Germany: the Russians bring tanks into East Berlin to put down public demonstrations.
18 Korea: ROKs release 27,000 NK POWs who refuse repatriation. Communists again break off truce talks.

25 Korea: CCF sends three armies totalling 100,000 troops, against five ROK divisions of half that number. The CCF assault is stopped

Algerian Emergency starts **1954**
Warsaw Pact created 14 May **1955**
Suez Crisis: Second Arab-Israeli War **1956**
Hungarian uprising 23 October **1956**
Aden Emergency starts (ends 1967) **1958**
Fidel Castro deposes Batista regime in Cuba **1959**

Trooper R.R Richardson (left) and Segeant F.W Andrews, Britons fighting with the United Nations forces in Korea, waiting in their armoured car for orders to move.

by a staggering UN artillery barrage of almost three million rounds.

July 1953
Cuba: Fidel Castro gaoled after abortive coup.

10 Korea: Truce talks resume.

24 Korea: The Chinese launch heavy attacks on The Hook.

26 Korea: A truce is finally signed at Panmunjon.

August 1953
31 Iran: Struggle for power between Mossadegh and the Shah leads to the former being ousted and jailed.

September 1953
Korea: Repatriation of POWs starts at Freedom Village, Panmunjom.

October 1953
British Guyana: Britain sends forces to forestall a coup.
Indo-China: Navarre's attack on Phu Ly held by Giap.
Israel: IDF paratrooper unit 101 under Ariel Sharon killed 69 civilians and destroy property in a raid on the Jordanian village of Qibieh. The raid was a reprisal for a raid on Tirat Yehuda.

November 1953
Indo-China: Navarre decides to construct base at Dien Bien Phu. Giap invades Laos again.

29 Vietnam: French forces capture Dien Bien Phu.

1950-1959

- Korean War starts on 25 June **1950**
- Chinese invade Tibet **1950**
- Indo-Chinese (Vietnam) War starts **1951**
- Korean war ends 26 July **1953**
- Mau Mau Emergency in Kenya starts (ends 1955) **1953**
- Cyprus Emergency starts (ends 1962) **1954**

Lieutenant-Colonel James Carne, VC, DSO, of the Gloucestershire Regiment, who commanded at the Imjin River battle in Korea, leads officers and men through Westgate St, Gloucester,.

1954

February 1954
Kenya: Establishment of British War Council.

March 1954
Indo-China: Giap begins attack on Dien Bien Phu.

April 1954
Kenya: Troubles continue, with the arrest of more than 20,000 suspects as mass surrender of Mau Mau is sought after capture of 'General' Katanga and surrender of 'General' Tanganyika.
Cyprus: Terrorist bombings begin, the work of EOKA—a pro 'Union with Greece' organisation, led by General Grivas.
Kenya: Henderson and Ruck contact Mau Mau leaders on Mount Kenya. Operation 'Anvil' on Nairobi. Development of pseudo-gangs and forest operating companies.
Algeria: CRUA formed.

May 1954
Indo-China: Dien Bien Phu falls. First Geneva Conference starts.

June 1954
Cyprus: Announcement that the British HQ in Suez Canal Zone will be moved to the island.

July 1954
Egypt: Large numbers of British troops pull out of the Canal Zone
Morocco: Anti French riots break out.
Israel-Egypt: The 'Lavon Affair': Israeli government spies, seemingly without PM's knowledge, make a failed attempt to sabotage British and US property in Egypt and put blame on Egyptian terrorists.

Algerian Emergency starts **1954** | Warsaw Pact created 14 May **1955** | Suez Crisis; Second Arab-Israeli War **1956** | Hungarian uprising 23 October **1956** | Aden Emergency starts (ends 1967) **1958** | Fidel Castro deposes Batista regime in Cuba **1959**

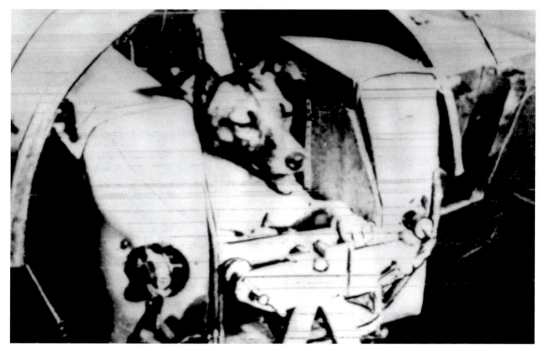

Laika, the Soviet satelilite dog, in her air conditioned kennel before being put into Sputnik II for her journey into space.

21 Indo-China: Armistice signed at Geneva. The agreement stipulates that the 17th parallel is only a provisional military demarcation line and general elections are to be held under international supervision in July 1956.

August 1954
Morocco: Anti-French riots break out.
Vietnam: US President Eisenhower approves policy of giving direct support to Diem in South, bypassing the French.

September 1954
8 Southeast Asia: SEATO is founded, eight nations signing a defence pact in Manila.

October 1954
Algeria: GRUA meeting in Switzerland plans campaign to start November 1 and changes its name to FLN.
Vietnam: French troops leave North.
Middle East: Agreement between Britain and Egypt for withdrawal of British troops from Suez Canal Zone and maintenance of civilian-manned base there.

31 Algeria: a rebellion against French rule begins, organised by the FLN.

November 1954
Cyprus: Greece raises Cyprus question in UN General Assembly. Grivas smuggled in in caique Siren. Caique St George intercepted, attempting to smuggle in arms.
Algeria: FLN campaign of violence starts with limited success. French 25th Airborne Division arrives and launches offensive in Aures Mountains.
Vietnam: General Lawton Collins appointed Eisenhower's Special Representative with Diem.

1950-1959

- Korean War starts on 25 June **1950**
- Chinese invade Tibet **1950**
- Indo-Chinese (Vietnam) War starts **1951**
- Korean war ends 26 July **1953**
- Mau Mau Emergency in Kenya starts (ends 1955) **1953**
- Cyprus Emergency starts (ends 1962) **1954**

15 Egypt: Najib dismissed as President of Egypt and is placed under house arrest. Nasser takes over as President

King Hussein of Jordan in the cockpit of a Vampire T.11 jet trainer during his visit to RAF Biggin Hill in Kent as part of his official visit to Britain with his wife Queen Dina.

1955

January 1955
Algeria: The FLN perpetrate massacres in various towns as they build up their guerrilla forces, tying down many French troops.
Kenya: Mau Mau members are offered an amnesty and simulataneously Operation 'Hammer' is launched in Aberdare Mountains.
Israel: Continuous incidents between Israel, Egypt and Syria, primarily in Gaza DMZ.

February 1955
Kenya: Operation 'First Flute' on Mount Kenya. Negotiations with Stanley Mathenge.
Algeria: Soustelle succeeds Léonard as Governor-General.
Israel: Israel launches Operation 'Black Arrow'

following Egyptian incursions, resulting in a major embarrassment for the Egyptian military and forcing Nasser to rethink his strategy with Israel.

24 Turkey and Iraq sign the British-sponsored Baghdad Pact. (They are joined by Pakistan and Iran later in the year.) The purpose of the Central Treaty Organisation (CENTO) is security against the USSR.
28 Middle East: Israeli forces kill 36 soldiers in a lightning raid on the Egyptian-held Gaza Strip.

April 1955
Middle East: A neutral zone is established in Jerusalem by Israel and Jordan.
South Vietnam: Civil war breaks out

Algerian Emergency starts 1954 · **Warsaw Pact created 14 May 1955** · **Suez Crisis: Second Arab-Israeli War 1956** · **Hungarian uprising 23 October 1956** · **Aden Emergency starts (ends 1967) 1958** · **Fidel Castro deposes Batista regime in Cuba 1959**

Picture dated december 1969 of Libyan Head of State Colonel Moamer Kadhafi (L) and Egyptian President Gamal Abdel Nasser (R, 1918-70) arriving together in Rabat prior the Arab Summit Conference.

between the government and the quasi-religious Binh Xuyen faction.
Kenya: General Lathbury succeeds Erskine as C-in-C.

1 Cyprus: EOKA campaign starts with bomb attacks.

May 1955
Cyprus: The EOKA attempt to blow up Governor, Sir Robert Armitage, fails.

14 Eastern Europe: The Warsaw Pact comes into existence, signed by the USSR and seven other communist countries for mutual defence.

15 Austria: The Allied occupation ends.

June 1955
Cyprus: The British invite Greek and Turkish Governments to Conference.
Vietnam: Ho Chi Minh's pressure for discussions on elections meets with no response.

July 1955
Morocco: The French proclaim martial law.
Malaya: First Federal elections held. Sweeping victory of Alliance Party, led by Tunku Abdul Rahman.
Kenya: Operation 'Dante' in Kiambu District.
Cyprus: Detention introduced. Evangelakis and Drakos arrested. Grivas moves from Nicosia to Troodos Mountains.

August 1955
Egypt: Nasser sets up a secret commando training school at Khan Unis; the Israelis attack it.
Cyprus: EOKA bomb attacks increase. Constable Poullis killed. Caraolis arrested and Georgadjis detained.

1950-1959

- Korean War starts on 25 June **1950**
- Chinese invade Tibet **1950**
- Indo-Chinese (Vietnam) War starts **1951**
- Korean war ends 26 July **1953**
- Mau Mau Emergency in Kenya starts (ends 1955) **1953**
- Cyprus Emergency starts (ends 1962) **1954**

(L-R:) Soviet leader Nikolai Aleksandrovich Bulganin, US President Dwight D. Eisenhower, French Premier Minister Edgar Faure and the British Prime Minister Sir Anthony Eden.

Algeria: Philippeville massacres lead to severe reprisals by French paras.

September 1955

Cyprus: A general strike is called, amid increasing violence. Garrison reinforced. Georgadjis, Evangelakis and Drakos escape from Kyrenia Castle and join Grivas.
Middle East: Israel accepts a UN cease-fire in the Gaza Strip, but clashes in Sinai continue. Egypt imposes blockade of Israeli shipping and concludes arms deal with Czechoslovakia.

19 Argentina: General Peron is overthrown and flees to Paraguay.

October 1955

Vietnam: After a referendum, Diem replaces Bao Daias President South Vietnam which is declared a republic.
Cyprus: Field Marshal Harding arrives as Governor and C-in-C. Meetings with Makarios.

November 1955

Cyprus: EOKA bomb attacks increase. First British serviceman murdered.

26 Cyprus: Bomb explosion in Ledra Palace Hotel, Nicosia. The British authorities declare of a state of emergency.

December 1955

Malaya: Meeting of Tunku Abdul Rahman, David Marshall and Chin Peng.
Cyprus: Operation 'Foxhunter' in Troodos Mountains. Search of monasteries. Haralambos Mouskos killed in ambush of Major Combe.

11 Israel: Israel launches an attack on Syria following provocation.

Algerian Emergency starts **1954**
Warsaw Pact created 14 May **1955**
Suez Crisis: Second Arab-Israeli War **1956**
Hungarian uprising 23 October **1956**
Aden Emergency starts (ends 1967) **1958**
Fidel Castro deposes Batista regime in Cuba **1959**

Cuban Defense Minister Raul Castro (L) talks with his brother Cuban President Fidel Castro (R) while watching a military parade 02 December.

1956

January 1956
Cuba: Insurgents under Fidel Castro attack rural police stations.

15 Cyprus: British reinforcements are sent to the island, and the EOKA leader, Archbishop Makarios, is banished, leading to protest riots.

February 1956
Algeria: Governor-General Soustelle replaced by Lacoste. Gen Lorillot replaces Gen Cherrire and Maj-Gen Massu arrives with 10th Para Div.

March 1956
India: China starts to build road in Aksai Chin. Khampa rebellion in Tibet.
Algeria: French troops are airlifted in.
Cyprus: Turkish Cypriots riot and loot Greek Cypriot shops.

1 Cyprus: Makarios meets with Lennox-Boyd and Harding, while Grivas explodes bombs.

5 Cyprus: EOKA attempt to blow up RAF Hermes fails.

9 Cyprus: Makarios, Bishop of Kyrenia, Ioarmides and Papastavros deported to Seychelles.

20 Cyprus: EOKA attempt to assassinate governor Harding fails.

28 S Vietnam: The last French troops leave Saigon.

1950-1959

- Korean War starts on 25 June **1950**
- Chinese invade Tibet **1950**
- Indo-Chinese (Vietnam) War starts **1951**
- Korean war ends 26 July **1953**
- Mau Mau Emergency in Kenya starts (ends 1955) **1953**
- Cyprus Emergency starts (ends 1962) **1954**

The Red Star is prominent over this square - flanked by Parliament and the Communist Party headquarters - scene of heavy fighting in Budapest, the capital, during the so-called Hungarian October Revolution.

April 1956

Algeria: More French troops are airlifted in.

5 Israel: Increased tension between Israel and Egypt-Syria. The IDF claim 180 attacks on Israel from Gaza in the past four months. Tit for tat raids and killings then culminate in an artillery duel and an Israeli artillery barrage targeting Gaza City that kills 59. Egypt responds by stepping up fedayeen commando raids that kill 12.

7 Morocco: Granted independence from France.

22 Aden: British troops clash with Yemenis on the border.

May 1956

Yemen: The Imam of Yemen concludes agreements with Egypt, Saudi Arabia and USS, to supply modern weapons.
Cyprus: First EOKA men, convicted of murder, hanged. Grivas announces death of two British Army deserters held by EOKA. Operation 'Pepperpot' in Troodos Mountains.
Algeria: Palestro incident: ambush and mutilation of French reservists. Massacre by FLN at Melouza.

10 Middle East: UN-sponsored cease-fire arranged between Israel and its Arabs.

June 1956

Poland: Martial law is proclaimed in Poznan after riots. Tanks are brought in and street fighting breaks out.
Cyprus: Operation 'Lucky Alphonse' round Kykko. Grivas narrowly escapes capture; moves to Limassol.
Algeria: Execution of FLN men, convicted of

Algerian Emergency starts **1954** | Warsaw Pact created 14 May **1955** | Suez Crisis; Second Arab-Israeli War **1956** | Hungarian uprising 23 October **1956** | Aden Emergency starts (ends 1967) **1958** | Fidel Castro deposes Batista regime in Cuba **1959**

The Prince of Wales inspecting the Guard of Honour drawn from the 2nd Battalion, 19th Punjab Regiment (Indian Army). The Prince visited the Protectorate during his voyage to India and the Far East.

murder, leads to fighting in Algiers.
Israel: Sharett resigns as Israeli PM and Golda Meir takes over.

15 Egypt: British troops leave the Canal Zone.

26 Egypt: Nasser seizes the Suez Canal from the Anglo-French company who run it.

July 1956
Cyprus: Lord Radcliffe starts constitutional inquiry.
Israel: The US withdraws funding from the Aswan dam, USSR steps in.
6 Middle East: Nasser announces the nationalisation of Suez Canal.

26 Egypt: Nasser nationalizes the Suez Canal Company and is supported by the Arab League. However Iraqi leaders secretly call on the British to topple Nasser . Martial law in Iraq.

30 UK: A ban is imposed on the export of war supplies to Egypt,

August 1956
Algeria: FLN conference in Soummam valley forms CCE and CNRA, tightens up the organisation and plans future campaign.

Cyprus: EOKA offers to suspend operations to enable discussions to start.
3 UK: 20,000 army reservists are called up. All Egyptian assets in Britain are frozen. Britain, France and Israel decide that the only way to ensure free passage through the Suez Canal is to capture it by force of arms .

23 Cyprus: Grivas rejects British terms. Nicos Sampson rescues Georgadjis.

1950-1959

- Korean War starts on 25 June **1950**
- Chinese invade Tibet **1950**
- Indo-Chinese (Vietnam) War starts **1951**
- Korean war ends 26 July **1953**
- Mau Mau Emergency in Kenya starts (ends 1955) **1953**
- Cyprus Emergency starts (ends 1962) **1954**

Strung out close to the buildings, an Allied patrol moves through an almost deserted street in Port Said, key town at the northern end of the Suez Canal.

September 1956

Algeria: FLN under Yacef increase violence in Algiers.

21 Middle East: Meeting at Villacoublay between French, British and Israelis to co-ordinate action on Suez Canal.

October 1956

Jordan: King Hussein dismisses General Glubb and all British officers of the Arab Legion.
Kenya: Dedan Kimathi killed. Army withdrawn from operations.
Cyprus: EOKA increase murders.
Middle East: British 16th Parachute Brigade removed to take part in Suez operation.
Algeria: Massu's 10th Parachute Division withdrawn to take part in Suez operation.

22 Algeria: FLN leaders including Ben Bella are arrested in Algiers.

23 Hungary: The Hungarian Uprising. The revolt against communism is led by liberal Prime Minister Imre Nagy, who informs the USSR that Hungary will leave the Warsaw Pact and introduce a multi-party system.

29 Egypt: Israeli paratroopers drop into the Mitla Pass, 30 miles from the Suez Canal, as a preliminary to Operation 'Musketeer'. The Israeli campaign in Sinai and the Gaza Strip begins.
Israel: Suez Campaign. In retaliation for a series of escalating border raids as well as the closure of the straits of Tiran and Suez canal to Israeli shipping, and to prevent Egyptian use of newly acquired Soviet arms in a war, Israel invades the Sinai peninsula and occupies it for several months, with collaboration of French and British interested in reversing the canal's nationalization. Israel withdraws after a UN

Algerian Emergency starts **1954** | Warsaw Pact created 14 May **1955** | Suez Crisis: Second Arab-Israeli War **1956** | Hungarian uprising 23 October **1956** | Aden Emergency starts (ends 1967) **1958** | Fidel Castro deposes Batista regime in Cuba **1959**

British paratroopers, alert and with their weapons ready, sit on a captured Russian-built, Egyptian Army tank at Port Said.

peace keeping force is placed in Sinai, and US guarantees right of passage for Israeli shipping through the Straits of Tiran.

30 Egypt: Britain and France issue an ultimatum to both Egypt and Israel, to withdraw their forces to ten miles from the Suez Canal. Nasser rejects the ultimatum.

31 Egypt: Operation 'Musketeer', the capture of the Suez Canal by British and French forces, begins with sea and air operations.
Hungary: Soviet forces withdraw from Budapest.

November 1956

Egypt: Israeli armour and paratroops fight a highly mobile lightning operation which reaches the Suez Canal in 100 hours.

4 Egypt: Israelis take Sharm el Sheik.
Hungary: Soviet forces with more than 1,000 tanks crush the uprising. UN calls for a Soviet withdrawal are ignored and Hungary is put under martial law.

5 Egypt: The first ground troops—1,000 British and French paratroops are dropped near Port Said. First helicopter assault.

6 Egypt: Seaborne assaults by British and French Commandos on Port Said and Port Fuad, with tank support. All objectives are taken and the operation is completely successful.

December 1956

Egypt: US and UN pressure forces UK and France to withdraw, to be replaced by UN.

28 Algeria: FLN murder the Mayor of Algeirs.

1950-1959

- Korean War starts on 25 June **1950**
- Chinese invade Tibet **1950**
- Indo-Chinese (Vietnam) War starts **1951**
- Korean war ends 26 July **1953**
- Mau Mau Emergency in Kenya starts (ends 1955) **1953**
- Cyprus Emergency starts (ends 1962) **1954**

SUEZ 1956: The only Suez airfield in Allied hands is at El Gamel, where British airborne troops made a landing during the first assault.

1957

January 1957

Egypt: Nasser tears up the Anglo-Egyptian Treaty of 1954 and denies Britain use of the Canal during wartime. When Israel withdraws from the Gaza Strip Egypt claims it and installs a governor, but is told it is under UN control.
Palestine: Fateh founded—with the express aim of destroying Israel.
Israel: The construction of Israel nuclear breeder reactor using French technology begins in Dimona. The French later try to stop the program, but back down when Israeli threatens to make the deal public.
Cyprus: Operations in Troodos Mountains result in death of Drakos and Afxentiou and recapture of Georgadjis. Sampson captured in Nicosia. Publication of Radcliffe's proposals.
Algeria: FLN cause a general strike; Massu moves 10th Parachute Division into Algiers.

16 Aden: invading Yemeni troops are scattered by British troops and aircraft.

February 1957
Algeria: Defeat of FLN in Casbah of Algiers. CCE leave Algiers and split up, Ben Bella and Belkacern Krim escaping to Tunisia.

March 1957
Cyprus: EOKA offer of cease-fire rejected.

April 1957
Cyprus: Makarios is released from the Seychelles and welcomed in Athens.

14 Jordan: King Hussein survives an attempted military coup led by General Abu Nuwar.

May 1957
Algeria: Fierce battles in Wilaya.

- Algerian Emergency starts **1954**
- Warsaw Pact created 14 May **1955**
- Suez Crisis: Second Arab-Israeli War **1956**
- Hungarian uprising 23 October **1956**
- Aden Emergency starts (ends 1967) **1958**
- Fidel Castro deposes Batista regime in Cuba **1959**

Their tame pigeon takes up its customary post on the Bren gun manned by this detachment of the Yorks and Lancs Regiment in the front line at El Cap on the Suez Canal, facing the Eqyptians.

June 1957
Algeria: Renewed FLN bomb attacks lead to return of French paras to Algiers.

July 1957
Oman: British troops move to suppress a rebellion against the Sultan.
Algeria: FLN meeting in Cairo forms a new CCE of five colonels and five politicals.

8 Eire: A state of emergency is declared against IRA terrorism.

August 1957
16 Oman: The rebel base at Nizwa is captured by British who then leave the country.

31 Malaya: Malaya becomes an independent state with Tunku Abdul Rahman as prime minister.

September 1957
Algiers: Final defeat of FLN in Casbah of Algiers. General strike by pieds noirs in Algiers, protesting at Lacoste's 'loi-cadre', suppressed by Massu's 10th Parachute Division.
India: China completes road through Aksai Chin.

15 Lebanon: Lebanese and Syrian troops clash on the border.

October 1957
Vietnam: Terrorist bombs kill US troops in Saigon.
USSR: Marshal Zhukov is dismissed from his post as minister of defence.

December 1957
Algeria: Abane murdered in Morocco on orders of Boussouf.

1950-1959

- Korean War starts on 25 June **1950**
- Chinese invade Tibet **1950**
- Indo-Chinese (Vietnam) War starts **1951**
- Korean war ends 26 July **1953**
- Mau Mau Emergency in Kenya starts (ends 1955) **1953**
- Cyprus Emergency starts (ends 1962) **1954**

demonstrators carry a banner reading 'Kampf dem Atomtod' (fight nuclear death) during a rally on Labour Day in Frankfurt, West Germany, 1 May 1958.

1958

January 1958
Aden: Governor declares a state of emergency.
30 Venezuela: Perez Jimenez is ousted in a coup by a civilian junta.

February 1958
Middle East: Egypt and Syria announce their merger into the United Arab Republic with Nasser as President. Egypt receives its first economic loan from USSR.
Iraq: Iraq and Jordan form a union
Tunisia: President Bourguiba demands the evacuation of all French troops.
Algeria: French bombing of Sakiet in Tunisia in retaliation for FLN raids across Morice line.

17 Campaign for Nuclear Disarmament (CND) founded in Britain to impede nuclear proliferation.

March 1958
Yemen: Yemen joins the UAR, alongside Egypt and Syria, with Nasser as President.

April 1958
Cyprus: EOKA renews its campaign of violence. Georgadjis escapes again. Inter-communal riots between Turks and Greeks.

May 1958
Algeria: FLN execution of three French soldiers leads to crisis and threatened coup by Salan and Massu. President Coty calls on de Gaulle, who assumes power in France. European colonists revolt.
France: General de Gaulle returns to power to prevent an army revolt.

Algerian Emergency starts **1954** | Warsaw Pact created 14 May **1955** | Suez Crisis; Second Arab-Israeli War **1956** | Hungarian uprising 23 October **1956** | Aden Emergency starts (ends 1967) **1958** | Fidel Castro deposes Batista regime in Cuba **1959**

Soviet leader Nikita Krushchev (C) arrives for a state visit in East Berlin, GDR, 7 August 1957. (L) Secretary General of the East German party SED Walter Ulbricht, and GDR Prime Minister Otto Grotewohl (2nd from L).

June 1958
Cyprus: The Greek v Turk conflict escalates.

July 1958
Iraq: Army coup led by Brigadier Kassem. King Faisal and his uncle, the crown prince, are shot, Prime Minister Nuri-es-Said is lynched and Kassem becomes president.
Egypt: Nasser signs new pact with Iraq.
Lebanon: Civil war breaks out.

16 Jordan: Following the Iraqi coup Jordan severs relations with the UAR. At the request of King Hussein, British paratroopers land.
Lebanon: USA sends in the marines.

29 Haiti: 'Papa Doc' Duvalier crushes an attempted coup and army rebellion.

August 1958
China: The Chinese attack the Nationalist island of Quemoy.

Cyrpus: Grivas calls for a cease-fire.

September 1958
Burma: General Ne Win ousts U Nu in a military coup.
Sri Lanka: The Tamils demand autonomy.
Cuba: Fidel Castro's guerrillas mount an all-out offensive.
Cyprus: Cease-fire called off.
Algeria: De Gaulle's constitutional referendum receives a 96 per cent 'Oui' from 80 per cent of Algerian electorate.

16 Algeria: FLN forms a provisional government.

October 1958
Pakistan: Martial law is proclaimed and General

1950-1959

- Korean War starts on 25 June **1950**
- Chinese invade Tibet **1950**
- Indo-Chinese (Vietnam) War starts **1951**
- Korean war ends 26 July **1953**
- Mau Mau Emergency in Kenya starts (ends 1955) **1953**
- Cyprus Emergency starts (ends 1962) **1954**

General Charles De Gaulle, wartime leader of the free French.

Ayub Khan becomes the new president.
Algeria: De Gaulle visits again: announces major concessions and, three weeks later, announces a 'paix des braves', with offer of amnesty to FLN.

December 1958
Cuba: Fidel Castro's guerrillas take Santiago.
Algeria: Salan removed; succeeded as Governor-General by Delouvrier and as C-in-C by General Challe, who plans systematic clearance operations.
India: Exchange of letters between Nehru and Chou En-lai over Tibetan frontier.

1959

Vietnam: Early in the year, Ho Chi Minh's government decides to assume control of opposition to Diem in the South and to renew armed struggle.

January 1959
Congo: The nationalist leader, Patrice Lumumba, is arrested.

2 Cuba: Fidel Castro sweeps in to power after the corrupt dictator Batista flees.

February 1959
Nyasaland (later Malawi): Riots by nationalists—British troops fly in.

19 Cyprus: International agreement is reached on the future of Cyprus. Makarios returns. Agreement reached in London for proposals for independent republic with British Sovereign Bases.

26 Southern Rhodesia (later Zimbabwe): A state of emergency is declared.

Algerian Emergency starts 1954 — **Warsaw Pact created 14 May 1955** — **Suez Crisis: Second Arab-Israeli War 1956** — **Hungarian uprising 23 October 1956** — **Aden Emergency starts (ends 1967) 1958** — **Fidel Castro deposes Batista regime in Cuba 1959**

The Australian and Swedish contingents in the anti-H bomb march from the Atomic Weapons Researcg Establishment at Aldermaston, Berkshire, to London.

March 1959
France: General de Gaulle takes French forces out of NATO.
Tibet: The Chinese invite the Dalai Lama to visit their HQ in Lhasa with the intention of taking him prisoner, but he manages to slip away. Kampa guerrillas continue to attack Chinese occupation forces.
Cyprus: Makarios returns. Grivas leaves. EOKA campaign ends.

24 Iraq: Iraq withdraws from its pact with Jordan.

June 1959
S Africa: Riots in Johannesburg over clearance of slum townships.

July 1959
Algeria: Operation 'Jumelles' begins in the Kabyle Mountains and continues until October.

August 1959
India: Clashes between Indian and China on disputed frontier in Ladakh and Assam.

29 India: Troops are sent to the border with China after incursions.

September 1959
Laos: A state of emergency is declared after the Pathet Lao attack army bases.
Algeria: FLN bombing campaign resuscitated; declaration of government in exile. de Gaulle announces new policy, leading to self-determination. Elements in French army begin to plot with the 'pieds noirs' to resist it.

November 1959
Rwanda-Burundi: Genocidal killings begin.

1960-1969

- Congo Emergency (ends 1965) **1960**
- Bay of Pigs **1961**
- Berlin Wall erected **1961**
- Cuba Missile Crisis **1962**
- Sino-Indian War **1962**
- Second Indo-Pakistan War **1965**

General Charles de Gaulle, President of France, salutes the memory of a great compatriot and fellow-soldier after placing a wreath on the Marshal Foch statue near Victoria Station, London.

Israel: Israel begins work on the National Water Carrier Project—to divert the waters of the River Jordan from the Sea of Galilee to the Negev, taking its share of the River Jordan water in accordance with the Johnston plan. Fierce Arab opposition results.

December 1959
14 Cyprus: Makarios elected Presiedent.

1960

January 1960
Algeria: European settlers rise in protest after de Gaulle dismisses General Jacques Massu. De Gaulle insists on Algerian self-determination.

31 Algeria: The settlers uprising subsides.

February 1960
Aden: Formation of Federation of Arab Amirates of the South, with British Defence Treaty.

March 1960
15 Congo: Martial law is proclaimed.

21 S Africa: Massacre in Sharpeville during PanAfrican Congress demonstrations. Leads to declaration of state of emergency on 30th.

April 1960
Algeria: Challe replaced by General Cripin.
India: Chou En-lai visits Delhi. Nehru orders forward policy on Tibetan frontier.

27 South Korea: Riots and civil disturbances lead to the resignation of Synghman Rhee.

May 1960
27 Turkey: Prime Minister Menderes is ousted in a military coup.

France leaves NATO **1966** | Third Arab-Israeli War: the Six-Day War **1967** | Biafran War **1967** | Soviet tanks enter Czechoslovakia **1968** | Tet Offensive in Vietnam **1968** | Northern Ireland Emergency starts **1969**

The Queen, with the Prime Ministers and heads of state attending the Commonwealth Prime Minister's Conference at the dinner party she gave a Buckingham Palace.

30 Congo: The country becomes independent, but simultaneously disintegrates into civil war.

June 1960
Algeria: Operation 'Tilsit', de Gaulle's abortive negotiation with Si Salah. Meeting at Melun between French Government and GRPA.

July 1960
Congo: The army mutinies.

11 Congo: Copper-rich Katanga secedes from the rest of the country.

August 1960
16 Cyprus: The island becomes independent.

September 1960
Congo: Colonel Joseph Mobutu takes over.
Cuba: Castro nationalises all US property.

October 1960
31 Malaya: After 12 years, the state of emergency is lifted.

November 1960
Congo: Congolese and UN troops clash.
Algeria: De Gaulle announces new policy, leading to Algerian Republic.
15 S Vietnam: A military coup fails.

December 1960
Algeria: Coup, planned to coincide with de Gaulle's visit, fails.
Vietnam: Civil war in Laos reaches crisis. Pressure for US intervention.

20 N Vietnam: The National Liberation Front (NLF) is formed to mastermind the take-over

1960-1969

Congo Emergency (ends 1965) **1960** | Bay of Pigs **1961** | Berlin Wall erected **1961** | Cuba Missile Crisis **1962** | Sino-Indian War **1962** | Second Indo-Pakistan War **1965**

US President John Kennedy and his wife Jacqueline are seen at the door of No.4, Buckingham Palace, London, as guests.

of S Vietnam.

31 Laos: Laos appeals to UN about N Vietnamese incursions.

1961

January 1961

2 Cuba: USA breaks off diplomatic relations with the Castro regime.

17 Congo: Patrice Lumumba is murdered in Katanga—fierce fighting between UN troops and pro-Lumumba supporters follows.

22 Congo: Belgian paratroopers fly into Stanleyville to rescue Europeans.

29 El Salvador: Military coup.

February 1961

Congo: It is agreed to form a federation of sov-ereign states in place of the existing republic.

April 1961

Angola: 500 whites are hacked to death during an uprising against Portuguese rule, starting the War of Independence.
Algeria: A coup, led by Challe, fails.

10 S Vietnam: President Ngo Dinh Diem wins elections. USA promises to increase military aid—including military advisers, substantially.

15 Ceylon (Sri Lanka): A state of emergency declared.

17 Cuba: Bay of Pigs invasion by Cuban exiles is defeated within three days by the troops of Castro

France leaves NATO **1966** | Third Arab-Israeli War: the Six-Day War **1967** | Biafran War **1967** | Soviet tanks enter Czechoslovakia **1968** | Tet Offensive in Vietnam **1968** | Northern Ireland Emergency starts **1969**

President John Kennedy (right) with his wife (second left) Jacqueline, meet the Queen and the Duke of Edinburgh on the American President's visit to Britain.

22 Algeria: Revolt of the Generals, led by General Salan, with weapons being distributed among the white settlers by the OAS.

23 Algeria: de Gaulle assumes dictatorial powers in France and the Algerian revolt subsides.

May 1961
Malaya: Tunku Abdul Rahman proposes formation of Malaysia, incorporating Singapore, North Borneo, Brunei and Sarawak.
Vietnam: The cease-fire in Laos becomes effective. Second Geneva Conference.

1 Cuba: Castro declares Cuba a one-party state and abolishes elections.

16 South Korea: A miilitary coup launched.

30 Dominica: Dictator Trujillo is assassinated.

31 S Africa: The country quits the British Commonwealth and declares itself a republic.

June 1961
19 Kuwait: Great Britain ends its protectorate.

26 Kuwait: Iraq claims soveriegnty over Kuwait

31 Kuwait: British troops are flown to forestall any Iraqi invasion attempt.

July 1961
9 USSR: Khrushchev announces increases in military spending.

11 France: The four generals who led the Algerian revolt are sentenced to death in

1960-1969

- Congo Emergency (ends 1965) **1960**
- Bay of Pigs **1961**
- Berlin Wall erected **1961**
- Cuba Missile Crisis **1962**
- Sino-Indian War **1962**
- Second Indo-Pakistan War **1965**

Major Yuri Gagarin, the first man in space, advances to place a wreath on the tomb of Karl Marx in Highgate Cemetery, London., during the closing stages of his visit to London.

absentia.

16 Kenya: The former Mau Mau leader Jorno Kenyatta is freed from prison.

25 USA: President Kennedy calls for increased defence spending.

August 1961

Algeria: France ends a 30-day cease-fire which has been in existence while peace talks with Muslim rebels have been in progress.

1 Congo: Cyrille Adoula is appointed prime minister of the Congo

16 Germany: Work starts on the building of a wall between East and West Berlin, to prevent refugees from leaving the east.

September 1961

Ghana: Nkrumah sacks British head of army and takes over. He then arrests all opposition leaders, claiming they are plotting to kill him.

16 Congo: UN troops again attempt to crush Katangan rebels.

17 Turkey: Former prime minister, Adnan Menderes, executed by the new military rulers.

18 Dag Hammarskjold, Secretary-General of the United Nations, dies in an air crash.

29 Syria: A military coup against the UAR is attempted.

October 1961

Algeria: Unrest continues, with many deaths in the rioting that marks the seventh anniver-

France leaves NATO **1966** · Third Arab-Israeli War: the Six-Day War **1967** · Biafran War **1967** · Soviet tanks enter Czechoslovakia **1968** · Tet Offensive in Vietnam **1968** · Northern Ireland Emergency starts **1969**

US President John Kennedy waves a cheerful farewell to Londoners as, accompanied by Mr Harold Macmillian, the Prime Minister, he drives from Buckingham Palace to the Airport.

sary of the 1954 Muslim rebellion.
Vietnam: Pressure from Diem leads to visit of General Taylor, coinciding with Mekong floods. Taylor recommends despatch of 8,000 US troops and strengthening of Military Aid Group above current levels.
Germany: British and US tanks are confronting Soviet armour along the wall and tank traps are being built in the east.

9 S Vietnam: A state of emergency is declared as the Viet Cong swell the ranks of the NLF.

24 Malta: The island becomes independent.

31 Congo: Another offensive is mounted against the Katangan rebels.

November 1961
Vietnam: JFK approves despatch of airlift, increase of MAG to over 2,000 and extension of its role; but rejects provision of active US troops.

India: Chinese incursion in Chip Chap valley leads Nehru to intensify forward policy.

December 1961
Albania: The USSR breaks off diplomatic relations after having banished Albania from the Soviet bloc.

19 India: The Portuguese enclaves of Goa, Daman and Diu are seized by India.

1962

January 1962
Algeria: OAS bombing campaign shifts to France.

1960-1969

Congo Emergency (ends 1965) 1960
Bay of Pigs 1961
Berlin Wall erected 1961
Cuba Missile Crisis 1962
Sino-Indian War 1962
Second Indo-Pakistan War 1965

President John F Kennedy at his weekly Press conference in Washington as viewers in Britain and Europe saw him televised live via the communcations satellite Telstar.

February 1962
France: Riots in Paris over the Algerian question.
S Vietnam: An unsuccessful military coup attempted.
Aden: Britain announces that forces will be stationed in Aden permanently.
India: India establishes new posts on the McMahon line.

8 S Vietnam: American Military Assistance Command established under General Harkins.

March 1962
18 Algeria: Peace agreement signed.

April 1962
1 Iraq: Kurdish revolt.

May 1962
India: Indo-Chinese War: Sectarian violence breaks out in West Bengal.

June 1962
India: China reacts to Indian attempt to occupy Thag La ridge.

17 France: The OAS ends its terror campaign.

July 1962
India: Indian patrol in Galwan valley surrounded by Chinese.
West New Guinea (West Irian): With the UN acting as intermediary, the Dutch cede West Irian to Indonesia.
Vietnam: US servicemen increased to 5,500. Peace signed at Geneva ending Laos Civil War.

3 Algeria: General de Gaulle signs an agreement recognising Algerian independence. Ben Bella returns and becomes prime minister.

France leaves NATO **1966** | Third Arab-Israeli War: the Six-Day War **1967** | Biafran War **1967** | Soviet tanks enter Czechoslovakia **1968** | Tet Offensive in Vietnam **1968** | Northern Ireland Emergency starts **1969**

The American Ambassador, Mr David Bruce (right) and Britain's Prime Minister Mr Harold MacMillan exchange a cordial handshake at the door of Admiralty House, Whitehall, London.

September 1962

Aden: Death of Imam of Yemen, followed by revolution, supported by Egypt.
Borneo: First elections in Brunei lead to victory of Partai Ra'ayat.

15 Algeria: Independence granted.

24 Aden: South Arabian Federation formed, opposed by Yemen. British troops quell riots.

27 Yemen: Imam Ahmed assassinated and a republic is established. Continual unrest between factions and with Aden (South Arabian Federation).

October 1962

11 Indo-Chinese War: Fighting breaks out on the Sino-Indian border (known as the McMahon Line) in the mountainous region between Tibet and India. India's further attempt to occupy Thag La ridge coincides with Chinese offensive in Assam and Ladakh. Ithe ndians withdraw.

15 UK: Amnesty International formed.

20 Indo-Chinese War: Chinese attack first and easily defeat the Indians.
22 Cuban Missile Crisis: President Kennedy announces the presence of Soviet missiles in Cuba. Castro refuses to allow UN inspection.

23 Indo-Chinese War: Taweng evacuated by India as Chinese press forward, launching a two-pronged offensive in the Aksai Chin area.

28 Cuban Missile Crisis: USSR defuses stand off situation by agreeing to dismantle missile sites.

1960-1969

- Congo Emergency (ends 1965) **1960**
- Bay of Pigs **1961**
- Berlin Wall erected **1961**
- Cuba Missile Crisis **1962**
- Sino-Indian War **1962**
- Second Indo-Pakistan War **1965**

November 1962

8 Indo-Chinese War: A cease-fire proposed by China is rejected by India.

14 Indo-Chinese War: India mounts an unsuccessful counter-offensive.

21 Indo-Chinese War: China, rather than invade Assam, declares a cease-fire withdraws behind the original McMahon Line.

December 1962

8 Borneo: Azahari launches TNKU revolt against Sultan of Brunei. British troops flown in from Singapore.

12 Borneo: British troops quell TNKU revolt. General Walker assumes command in North Borneo, Brunei and Sarawak.

29 Congo: UN troops occupy the Katangan capital of Elisabethville.

Scene of turmoil and confusion outside the United States Embassy (background), London, as crowds of placard-carrying demonstrators pressed forward against a strong police cordon at the top of the Embassy steps.

1963

January 1963

Aden: Aden Colony joins South Arabian Federation. Border clashes with Yemen.

1 Congo: President Tshombe appeals to the UN to declare a cease-fire. He is put under house arrest by the UN on the 8th.

13 Togo: A military coup takes place.

15 Congo: Tshombe bows to UN pressure and announces the end of the Katangan seccession.

16 Tunisia: An attempt to assassinate President Bourguiba fails and 13 are sentenced to death.

France leaves NATO **1966** | Third Arab-Israeli War: the Six-Day War **1967** | Biafran War **1967** | Soviet tanks enter Czechoslovakia **1968** | Tet Offensive in Vietnam **1968** | Northern Ireland Emergency starts **1969**

February 1963
8 Iraq: A military coup ousts and executes Abd el-Karim Kassem, replacing him with Colonel Arif.

10 Iraq: The Iraqi army resumes operations against the Kurds.

March 1963
Syria: A military coup brings the Baath Party to power.
31 Guatemala: President Fuentes overthrown.

April 1963
Borneo: Indonesian attack on Tebedu police station.

May 1963
8 S Vietnam: President Dinh Diem's troops fire on Bhuddist demonstrators in Hue. Henry Cabot Lodge replaces Nolting as US Ambassador. Threatened coup against Diem by Big Minh. There is then a reappraisal of US policy.

On this day in history, President John F Kennedy tells the world that the USA is to blockade the Island of Cuba to stop them from completing a Russian Missile Complex, 80 miles from the American mainland

June 1963
6 Iran: Severe riots follow the arrest of the Imam Khomeini. Martial law proclaimed.

11 S Vietnam: a Bhuddist priest burns himself to death in protest and this is followed by similar suicides.

August 1963
USA: A telephone 'hotline' is established between the USA and USSR to prevent future crises escalating.
Borneo: Indonesian raids in First and Third Division of Sarawak.

22 S Vietnam: Diem raids Bhuddist temples and proclaims martial law.

1960-1969

- Congo Emergency (ends 1965) **1960**
- Bay of Pigs **1961**
- Berlin Wall erected **1961**
- Cuba Missile Crisis **1962**
- Sino-Indian War **1962**
- Second Indo-Pakistan War **1965**

US Defence Secretary Robert McNamara (L) tells reporters that he supported an increase of NATO air strikes against Yugoslavia.

September 1963
Vietnam: US Defence Secretary McNamara and General Taylor on fact-finding mission.

16 Malaysia: The Federation of Malaysia formed—consisting of Malaya, Singapore, North Borneo and Sarawak. Civil unrest swiftly follows. British Embassy at Djakarta attacked and burned. Indonesian attack on LongJawi.
18 Malaysia: Martial law proclaimed.

25 Dominican Republic: The government is overthrown.

October 1963
Algeria: Border issues with Morocco—10,000 troops launch an offensive against Algeria.
Syria: Syria forms military alliance with Iraq.
Aden: NLF launches revolutionary struggle.

3 Honduras: The president is overthrown by a military coup.

30 Algeria: Cease-fire is agreed between Algeria and Morocco.

November 1963
1 S Vietnam: With tacit American support, a group officers overthrow and murder Diem.

4 Germany: Soviet troops blockade a US convoy attempting to reach West Berlin.

18 Iraq: A military anti-Baathist coup overthrows the Arif government.

22 USA: President Kennedy is assassinated.

December 1963
Aden: Bomb attack on governor, Sir Kennedy Trevaskis, at airfield. State of Emergency declared.
Borneo: Indonesian attack on Kalabakan.

France leaves NATO **1966** | Third Arab-Israeli War: the Six-Day War **1967** | Biafran War **1967** | Soviet tanks enter Czechoslovakia **1968** | Tet Offensive in Vietnam **1968** | Northern Ireland Emergency starts **1969**

10 Aden: A state of emergency declared after grenades are thrown at Aden airport. The frontier is closed and 100 Yemenis are rounded up and deported.

12 Kenya: Kenya becomes independent with Kenyatta as its prime minister.

21 Cyprus: Clashes between Greeks and Turks.

1964

January 1964

Panama: Anti-American riots erupt.
Aden: Britain proposes a self-governing federation with independence in 1968. Three groups oppose the federal government: NLF (National Liberation Front), FLOSY (Front for the Liberation of South Yemen) and the South Arabian League. All plus Yemen, cause continual problems involving the British Army, the FRA (Federal Regular Army) and the FNG (Federal

(Left) Jacqueline Kennedy, widow of US President John F. Kennedy, leaves the Capitol building.
(Above) Presiden Kennedy waves as he leaves the Buckingham Palace for the US Embassy.

National Guard) in operations, such as 'Nutcracker' in the Radfan during January.
Borneo: Cease-fire during talks in Bangkok.
S Vietnam: Fighting between the S Vietnamese Army and the Viet Cong becomes more severe and more appeals for help are made to the USA.
Uganda: British troops fly in to crush a military mutiny.
Zanzibar: the Sultan is overthrown by nationalists who declare a 'People's Republic'

13–17 Egypt: Arab summit held in Cairo—prompted by concerns about Israel's River Jordan diversion scheme. A Unified Arab Command under Egyptian supervision is created.

1960–1969

Congo Emergency (ends 1965) **1960** | Bay of Pigs **1961** | Berlin Wall erected **1961** | Cuba Missile Crisis **1962** | Sino-Indian War **1962** | Second Indo-Pakistan War **1965**

Secretary of Defense McNamara and General Westmoreland, Vietnam Assistance Command Commander, talks with General Tee on the condition of the war in Vietnam.

February 1964

Cyprus: More vicious fighting between Greeks and Turks breaks out.

5 Rwanda: Thousands of members of the Tutsi tribe are massacred.

March 1964

Aden: Cross border air attacks. Further operations (including SAS) are launched in the Radfan.
Borneo: Battle of Kling Klang ridge.

April 1964

19 Laos: Right-wing army officers topple the government in a coup.

22 Zanzibar: 'Act of Union' is declared between Zanzibar and Tanganyika.

May 1964

Palestine: PLO (Palestine Liberation Organization) founded. The Palestinian National Charter calls for the annihilation of Israel.
British Guyana: Troops are sent from Britain after civil unrest in May, and a state of emergency is declared.
Aden: British troops reinforced.
India: Nehru dies; succeeded by Shastri.

June 1964

S Rhodesia: Ian Smith warns Britain that he will declare UDI if relations worsen.
Aden: Operations in the Radfan end.
Vietnam: Taylor succeeds Lodge as US Ambassador. General Westmoreland succeeds Harkins as commander of US Military Aid Command. General Khanh seizes power from Big Minh.

3 South Korea: Martial law is proclaimed after severe rioting.

France leaves NATO **1966** — Third Arab-Israeli War: the Six-Day War **1967** — Biafran War **1967** — Soviet tanks enter Czechoslovakia **1968** — Tet Offensive in Vietnam **1968** — Northern Ireland Emergency starts **1969**

Ian Smith, Prime Minister of Rhodesia.

July 1964
Aden: Britain announces intention to maintain a military base in Aden, but to grant independence to South Arabia not later than 1968.

August 1964
Cyprus: After more unrest including a threatened invasion by Turkey, a UN force is sent in to divide the warring factions.
S Vietnam: The 'Americanisation' of the war begins with US troops arriving in force.
Borneo: Indonesia launches naval and airborne attacks against Malayan mainland.
Vietnam: The Gulf of Tonkin incident leads to US Congressional Resolution giving the President the authority to use armed force.

10 Cyprus: A UN truce is brokered.

September 1964
Vietnam: UN Secretary General U Thant tries to arrange a meeting between US and North Vietnam. Rejected by US. Coup attempted against Khanh. Revolt of Montagnards.

3 Malaysia: Landings by Indonesian units in Central Malaysia are repulsed. Confrontation with Indonesian forces also begins in Sarawak, North Borneo (Sabah) and Brunei.

13 Egypt: Second Arab Summit. Held at Alexandria, it decides on the diversion of the headwaters of the Jordan as well as strengthening regional Arab armies with the ultimate aim of destroying Israel.

October 1964
15 USSR: Khrushchev ousted by Leonid Brezhnev in 'Kremlin coup'.

1960-1969

- Congo Emergency (ends 1965) **1960**
- Bay of Pigs **1961**
- Berlin Wall erected **1961**
- Cuba Missile Crisis **1962**
- Sino-Indian War **1962**
- Second Indo-Pakistan War **1965**

Vietcong soldiers climbing onto a US tank abandoned on a road in Hue in 1968 during the Tet general offensive.

November 1964

S Vietnam: S Vietnamese forces launch their largest attack to date, aimed at a Viet Minh stronghold in the jungle some 40 miles NW of Saigon—7,000 troops are involved, supported by 105 US Army helicopters.
Aden: The NLF steps up its campaign of violence.
Borneo: Operation 'Claret'—across Indonesian border, is authorised.

2 Saudi Arabia: King Saud is deposed.

26 Congo (Zaire): Belgian paratroopers land at the capital, Stanleyville (Kisangani), to protect white settlers.

December 1964

Aden: British 24th Infantry Brigade completes the move from Kenya to Little Aden.
Borneo: British reinforcements bring Walker's command up to 14,000 men.
Vietnam: Increase in Vietcong attacks, including USAF bases. Reconsideration of US policy. Johnson decides on Operation 'Rolling Thunder', bombing campaign against North.

1965

January 1965

Vietnam: Ho Chi Minh and Giap decide plan of major intervention by NVA to concentrate round Saigon, aiming for victory by 1968.
India: Elections in Pakistan. Clash between Indian and Pakistani police in Rann of Kutch.

2 Indonesia: Indonesia quits the UN.

24 UK: Winston Churchill dies.

France leaves NATO **1966**
Third Arab-Israeli War: the Six-Day War **1967**
Biafran War **1967**
Soviet tanks enter Czechoslovakia **1968**
Tet Offensive in Vietnam **1968**
Northern Ireland Emergency starts **1969**

A general view of the coffin and mourners entering St. Paul's Cathedral, London, for the funeral of Sir Winston Churchill.

February 1965
Vietnam: Generals Thieu and Ky oust Khanh. Bombing of the North starts. Westmoreland obtains authority to use US troops to defend air bases.

3 Gibraltar: Spain begins a blockade over the dispute of sovereignty.

7 Vietnam: The Viet Cong begin a major offensive in the Central Highlands.

22 India: Rising tension on the Sino-Indian border following Chinese troop movements.

March 1965
Indonesia: Suharto takes over from Sukarno.
Borneo: Walker hands over command to Maj-Gen Lea.

8 Vietnam: The first US combat troops land at Da Nang.

April 1965
Borneo: Indonesian attack on Plaman Mapu.
Vietnam: Johnson approves increase in US troop strength to 82,000, but limits their activity to fifty miles from 'enclaves'.
India: Pakistan attacks Rann of Kutch. Indians withdraw.

9 India: Indian forces invade the Rann of Kutch, fighting with Pakistan over the disputed border area.

25 Dominican Republic: The army ousts President Cabral and asks the USA for help against communists who have infiltrated the government.

27 Dominican Republic: The Organisation

1960-1969

- Congo Emergency (ends 1965) **1960**
- Bay of Pigs **1961**
- Berlin Wall erected **1961**
- Cuba Missile Crisis **1962**
- Sino-Indian War **1962**
- Second Indo-Pakistan War **1965**

A US Marine walks through a gully saturated with punji sticks 28 January, 1966, during a patrol in Vietnam.

of American States (OAS) sends in a multinational force led by US marines to help keep order.

May 1965
28 Rhodesia: A state of emergency is declared in various areas.

June 1965
Aden: Turnbull declares State of Emergency in Aden State and proscribes NLF.
Vietnam: Intervention of NVA leads Westmoreland to request increase in US troop strength from seventeen to forty-four battalions to save the South Vietnamese ARVN from defeat.
India: Agreement over Rann of Kutch reached between Ayub Khan and Shastri in London.
Dominican Republic: US marines are withdrawn.

7 Morocco: King Hassan imposes royal autocracy.

8 Vietnam: General Westmoreland announces that he will use US troops in offensive operations
18 Algeria: Ben Bella is ousted by Bournedienne.

July 1965
India: Pakistani irregulars infiltrate into Indian-held Kashmir.
USA: Johnson authorises the deployment of US Airmobile Cavalry Division and other troops, bringing the total to 125,000. Later he agrees to total increase of 100,000 and lifts restrictions on their use. Conscription for service in Vietnam reaches 35,000 a month.

August 1965
Aden: Murder of police superintendent and Speaker of Assembly.

France leaves NATO **1966**
Third Arab-Israeli War: the Six-Day War **1967**
Biafran War **1967**
Soviet tanks enter Czechoslovakia **1968**
Tet Offensive in Vietnam **1968**
Northern Ireland Emergency starts **1969**

Borneo: Singapore leaves Malaysia.
Vietnam: US troops engaged in major operations in Central Highlands and coastal strip.

5 India: India claims Pakistani irregular infiltration in Kashmir to be a full-scale invasion.
24 India: India retaliates by sending troops across the cease-fire line in Kashmir.

September 1965
India: Indian counter-offensive in Punjab. War ends with cease-fire, called for by UN.

1 India: Pakistan responds by launching a brigade-sized attack in the Chamb area.

6 India: The Indians retaliate with a three pronged attack towards Lahore, Sialkot and Hyderabad.

23 Aden: A grenade is thrown at British schoolchildren at an airfield. Turnbull dismisses

Within the scope of Operation Double Eagle, a US Marines helicopter touches down on the central Vietnam coast in the Quang Ngai Province.

Mackawee and direct rule is then imposed by Britain.
India: A cease-fire comes into effect.

30 Indonesia: A communist coup to oust Sukarno fails, although a number of generals are murdered.

October 1965
Cuba: Castro announces that Che Guevara has left Cuba to fight 'imperialism abroad'.
Aden: Federal troops brought in to support British in Crater. PSP leaders arrested.
Borneo: A pro-communist coup in Indonesia leads to fighting between communists and their opponents.

18 Morocco: Third Arab Summit at

1960-1969

- Congo Emergency (ends 1965) **1960**
- Bay of Pigs **1961**
- Berlin Wall erected **1961**
- Cuba Missile Crisis **1962**
- Sino-Indian War **1962**
- Second Indo-Pakistan War **1965**

Casablanca. The conference drafts a plan to hold off from war until the build up Arab armed forces.

November 1965
11 Rhodesia: Ian Smith makes his long-threatened declaration of independence. The UN condemn it and Great Britain imposes sanctions, but decides against the use of military force, although they offer military aid to neighbouring Zambia.

25 Congo (Zaire): General Mobutu imposes military rule for five years.

31 Vietnam: There are now 165,700 US troops in Vietnam.

December 1965
24 Vietnam: Christmas truce is agreed, after China has agreed to increase aid to N Vietnam earlier in the month.

Che Guevara, theoretician and tactician of guerrilla warfare and prominent figure in Castro's revolution in Cuba. He left Cuba in 1965 to organize guerrilla fighters in Congo and later Bolivia. Captured and shot by the Bolivian army, he immediately achieved international fame and the status of a martyred hero.

1966

January 1966
S Vietnam: American troops are used in major 'search and destroy' operations for the first time.
Central African Republic: Colonel Jean Bokassa takes office after a coup.
Aden: OLOS combine with NLF to form FLOSY, SAL breaking away.
India: Russian-sponsored conference in Tashkent leads to withdrawal of Indian and Pakistani troops to pre-August 5 positions. Shastri dies, succeeded by Mrs Gandhi.

15 Nigeria: A military coup takes place and

France leaves NATO **1966** · Third Arab-Israeli War: the Six-Day War **1967** · Biafran War **1967** · Soviet tanks enter Czechoslovakia **1968** · Tet Offensive in Vietnam **1968** · Northern Ireland Emergency starts **1969**

Members of the 2nd and 4th Battalions of the 503 US Infantry and 173rd Airborne Brigade fight on Hill 875 and 886 at Dak To in South Vietnam in 1968.

General Ironsi is proclaimed head of state.

February 1966

Aden: Britain announces that she no longer intends to station British forces in South Arabia after independence in 1968.
Vietnam: Honolulu meeting to review US troop strength. Westmoreland's request to raise total to 429,000 men by the end 1966 reduced by McNamara to 367,000. Westmoreland warns of a long war.

24 Ghana: Nkrumah is overthrown.

March 1966

Belgium: NATO Headquarters moves to Brussels, after France removes her troops from NATO.
Borneo: General Suharto replaces Sukarno as ruler of Indonesia.
Vietnam: Internal fighting within ARVN round Danang and Hua lasts till May. Westmoreland launches attacks on NVA in 'War Zones' round Saigon. Increased NVA activity near 17th parallel demilitarized zone.

May 1966

Borneo: Discussions between Malaysia and Indonesia start, leading to meeting in Bangkok in June.
Vietnam: Extension of the offensive Operation 'Rolling Thunder' to include oil installations near Hanoi and Haiphong is authorised.

23 S Vietnam: Government troops take over Danang

June 1966

China: Red Guards advance the Cultural Revolution to re-invigorate the flagging revolu-

1960-1969

Congo Emergency (ends 1965) **1960** · Bay of Pigs **1961** · Berlin Wall erected **1961** · Cuba Missile Crisis **1962** · Sino-Indian War **1962** · Second Indo-Pakistan War **1965**

tionary process.
1 Indonesia: General Suharto confrontation with Malaysia signing a provisional agreement being signed in Bangkok.

16 S Vietnam: Government troops take Hue.

28 Argentina: A non-violent military coup topples the government

July 1966
Nigeria: General Ironsi is killed in another coup and replaced by Lt-Col Yakubu Gowon.
Borneo: Suharto finally strips Sukarno of all powers.
Vietnam: US Marines occupy Khe Sanh.

August 1966
11 Borneo: Peace agreement between Malaysia and Indonesia.

UH-1D helicopters airlift infantry from the Filhol Rubber Plantation area to a new staging area, during Operation "Wahiawa".

September 1966
6 S Africa: PM Verwoerd assassinated.

October 1966
Gibraltar: In Spain tightens its blockade.
Israel: Arab terrorist activities increase.
Vietnam: Johnson offers to withdraw US troops six months after NVA has done the same and ceased intervention in the South. Operation 'Attleboro' launched.

November 1966
S Vietnam: The Viet Cong shell Saigon

4 Egypt: Defence agreement with Syria is signed.

13 Israel: Israeli troops launch the Samu raid. Palestinians riot and clash with Jordanian security forces throughout West Bank, especially in

France leaves NATO **1966**
Third Arab-Israeli War: the Six-Day War **1967**
Biafran War **1967**
Soviet tanks enter Czechoslovakia **1968**
Tet Offensive in Vietnam **1968**
Northern Ireland Emergency starts **1969**

Nablus where the army intervenes. The PLO continues to gain support.

16 Jordan: Mobilisation is ordered after an Israeli punitive raid into Samu.

December 1966
Aden: NLF breaks with FLOSY.
22 Rhodesia: Ian Smith declares a republic.
Vietnam: By the end of the year US troop strength has reached 400,000.

1967

January 1967
Israel: Almost daily border raids and harassment from Arab terrorists are accompanied by obvious military preparations by Arab neighbours.
Vietnam: US troops launch a major offensive on the Viet Cong 'Iron Triangle' jungle stronghold.

A Viet Cong prisoner awaits interrogation at the A-109 Special Forces Detachment in Thuong Duc, Vietnam, (25 km west of Da Nang), 23 January 1967.

February 1967
Vietnam: USA mounts Operation 'Junction City' in the Tay Ninh and Binh Long provinces.
Aden: Major riots and violent incidents. NLF and FLOSY fight each other, notably in Sheikh Othman and Al Mansoura.

March 1967
Aden: Commonwealth Secretary, George Thomson, proposes independence brought forward to November 1967. Rejected by Federation. Serious rioting is followed by uprisings all over country.
Middle East: Gromyko visits Cairo.

31 Sierra Leone: A military coup.

April 1967
USA: In New York demonstrators protest against American involvement in Vietnam.

1960-1969

- Congo Emergency (ends 1965) **1960**
- Bay of Pigs **1961**
- Berlin Wall erected **1961**
- Cuba Missile Crisis **1962**
- Sino-Indian War **1962**
- Second Indo-Pakistan War **1965**

Vietnam: On visit to USA, Westmoreland requests increase in troop strength to 670,000 and authority to extend operations into Laos, Cambodia and North Vietnam. Request reduced to 525,000 and extensions refused.
Middle East: Land and air clashes between Israeli and Syrian forces.
Aden: Visit by Lord Shackleton, proposing independence in January 1968, receives non-committal reply. Visit by the UN Mission is greeted by increased violence.

21 Greece: The colonels take over.

(Left) Reinforced by helicopters, US soldiers search for North Vietnamese guerillas.
(Above) US Soldiers near hill 875 and 886 at Dak To.

27 Egypt: Nasser cancels a planned Egyptian attack on Israel, after it becomes obvious that the Israelis were expecting it.

30 Egypt: Egypt signs a defence pact with Jordan.

31 Nigeria/Biafra: Colonel Ojukwu declares the eastern region (Biafra) to be an independent republic. This is rejected and civil war begins.

May 1967

Egypt: Egypt moves troops into Sinai and blockades the Straits of Tiran.
Middle East: Syria mobilizes. On demand of Egypt, UN Force withdrawn from Sinai, except Sharm el Sheikh and Gaza strip. Israel and Egypt mobilize.

June 1967

Aden: 18 Britons murdered in a native police mutiny.
1 Israel: General Moshe Dayan is appointed defence minister.
Jordan joins Arab military alliance and agrees to an Iraqi division entering its borders.

France leaves NATO **1966**
Third Arab-Israeli War: the Six-Day War **1967**
Biafran War **1967**
Soviet tanks enter Czechoslovakia **1968**
Tet Offensive in Vietnam **1968**
Northern Ireland Emergency starts **1969**

Former Israeli Prime Minister David Ben-Gurion (l) accompanied by Israeli defence minister General Moshe Dayan (r).

5 Middle East: the Six Day War begins with Israeli pre-emptive air strikes on Egypt, Jordan and Syrian air force bases, followed by attacks into Sinai, West Bank, Jerusalem and Syria. Jordan shells Israeli areas of Jerusalem.

7 Middle East: : Israeli forces capture Gaza strip, El Arish, Mitla and Gidi Passes in Sinai. Jordanian forces withdraw to the East Bank.
9 Middle East: Israeli forces reach Suez Canal and attack Syrian positions on Golan Heights.

10 Middle East: Cease-fire comes into effect. In six days the Israelis have captured Sinai, the Golan Heights, old Jerusalem and the West Bank, decimating the opposing Arab forces.

16 Aden: Mutiny in South Arabian Army leads to fighting between British troops and Aden Police in Crater, in which some British killed.

30 Aden: British troops occupy the Crater.

August 1967
Middle East: Khartoum Conference—The fourth Arab summit says no to peace or negotiations with Israel.

9 Nigeria: Biafran troops cross the River Niger and invade the rest of the country.

September 1967
Vietnam: Viet Cong begin major operations, while the Americans fortify Khesang.

3 Vietnam: General Nguyen Van Thieu becomes president of S Vietnam.

11 India: Another border clash with China.

1960-1969

- Congo Emergency (ends 1965) **1960**
- Bay of Pigs **1961**
- Berlin Wall erected **1961**
- Cuba Missile Crisis **1962**
- Sino-Indian War **1962**
- Second Indo-Pakistan War **1965**

Former Israeli Defence Minister Moshe Dayan (C) and Gen. Rechavam Zeevi (2nd, L) in conversation with the Palestinian keeper of the Cave of the Patriarchs in Hebron during the 1967 Six day war.

October 1967
USA: In Washington thousands protest against American involvement in Vietnam.
9 Bolivia: Che Guevara killed by Bolivian troops at Quebrada del Yuro.

21 Egypt: An Egyptian missile ship sinks the Israeli destroyer *Eilath*. Israel retaliates with an artillery bombardment of the Suez oil installations.
25 Peru: A military coup is mounted to oust the Belaunde government.

Vietnam: Operation 'Fairfax' begins in the area round Saigon.

30 Laos: Attacks launched by N Vietnamese troops.
31 Vietnam: There are now half a million Americans serving there.

November 1967
28 Aden: British forces are withdrawn after 128 years of colonial rule.

30 South Arabia becomes independent.

December 1967
Greece: The Colonels survive a counter-coup led by King Constantine who then flees the country.

1968

January 1968
Czechoslovakia: Premier Dubcek introduces a liberal regime. Warsaw Pact tanks are moved to the border.

31 Vietnam: Viet Minh launch the Tet Offensive attacking South Vietnamese cities and towns.

France leaves NATO **1966** — Third Arab-Israeli War: the Six-Day War **1967** — Biafran War **1967** — Soviet tanks enter Czechoslovakia **1968** — Tet Offensive in Vietnam **1968** — Northern Ireland Emergency starts **1969**

February 1968
Vietnam: General Wheeler visits and reviews strategy after Tet Offensive; supports Westmoreland's request for further 206,000 troops.

25 Vietnam: After 26 days of bitter fighting, Hue is recaptured by American and S Vietnamese forces.

March 1968
Falklands: Britain rejects Argentinian claim.
Vietnam: General Creighton Abrams replaces General Westmoreland in charge of US forces. Clifford Clark replaces McNamara as US Defence Secretary. Johnson consults the 'Wise Men', who recommend limiting the bombing of the North and troop reinforcements; and also advise opening negotiations with the North.

16 Vietnam: Massacre at My Lai by US troops.

Female Vietcong soldier in action with an anti-tank gun during a fighting in southern Cuu Long delta in the frame of the Tet general offensive launched in all the South Vietnam in spring 1968.

21 Middle East: Battle of Karameh—Jordanian and Palestinian forces repulse Israel's retaliatory raid on a Jordanian town that had served as a staging area for guerilla attacks and a base for PLO/Fatah.
31 Vietnam: Johnson announces he will not stand again. Discussions start on procedure for negotiations in Paris.

June 1968
Egypt: The Egyptians violate the cease-fire along the Suez canal.

July 1968
17 Iraq: A Baathist-led coup in Iraq.

August 1968
19 Nigeria: A major federal offensive opens,

1960-1969

Congo Emergency (ends 1965) **1960** | Bay of Pigs **1961** | Berlin Wall erected **1961** | Cuba Missile Crisis **1962** | Sino-Indian War **1962** | Second Indo-Pakistan War **1965**

but the Biafrans continue to fight tenaciously.

October 1968
21 Czechoslovakia: Warsaw Pact tanks move into Prague and are met by protesting students; the Czech Army does not resist on Dubcek's orders.

November 1968
Vietnam: In response to halt in US bombing, N Vietnam indicates it will not infringe DMZ nor attack major cities.

December 1968
Athens: PFLP attack on El Al plane killing an Israeli.

28 Israel: Response to the Athens attack is a helicopter raid on Beirut Airport; 13 Arab aircraft destroyed.

31 Vietnam: By the end of the year American troop strength is at 540,000.

On this day in 1968, US troops recapture the Vietnamese city of Hue after it had been taken the the Viet Cong during the Tet Offensive.

1969

January 1969
Vietnam: Nixon becomes President. Procedure for negotiations in Paris agreed.

February 1969
Vietnam: NVA and Vietcong renew offensive throughout South.
Syria: Internal struggles in Syrian Ba'th party: Hafez al-Assad, defense minister, takes full control over military in Syria; civilian institutions left under the control of President Atasi.

1–4 Egypt: Fifth Palestine National Council (PNC) in Cairo. Fatah gains formal control with Arafat declared chair of Executive Committee. The PNC statement sets the aim of a secular democratic state society for Muslims, Christians and Jews.

France leaves NATO **1966** | Third Arab-Israeli War: the Six-Day War **1967** | Biafran War **1967** | Soviet tanks enter Czechoslovakia **1968** | Tet Offensive in Vietnam **1968** | Northern Ireland Emergency starts **1969**

Jordanian soldiers carry a portrait of King Hussein in their jeep in this photo taken in June 1967.

18 Switzerland: PFLP attack El Al plane in Zurich.

20 Israel: PFLP bomb attack on a Jerusalem supermarket.

22 S Vietnam: Communists renew the offensive.

24 Syria: Israeli launches airstrikes against two al-Fatah camps near Damascus. Fatah moves to strengthen its position in Jordan; PFLP calls more explicitly for the overthrow of King Hussein, who is seen as a Western puppet.

March 1969

Vietnam: Vietcong rocket attacks on Saigon. In retaliation Nixon orders bombing of Viet Minh 'sanctuaries' in Cambodia.
Egypt: Military tension escalates along the Suez canal between Israel and Egypt. The Soviets supply SAM-2 radar and pilots to the Egyptians, US supplies Israel with Phantom jets and Hawk missiles.

2 China: Sino-Soviet border clash at the River Ussuri.

11 Israel: Golda Meir becomes Prime Minister in Israel after death of Levi Eshkol.

25 Pakistan: President Ayub Khan cedes power to the chief of the army.

April 1969

Nigeria: Biafran troops hold on thanks to military aid from France.

23 Nigeria: Government forces capture Umuahia.
Israel/Egypt: War of attrition. Constant artillery and air battles around the Suez canal,

1970-1979

- Third Indo-Pakistan War **1971**
- Bloody Sunday in Northern Ireland **1972**
- Fourth Arab-Israeli War **1973**
- Turks invade Cyprus **1974**
- Angolan Civil War **1975**
- Pol Pot and Khmer Rouge take Cambodia **1975**

Files released by the Public Record Office reveal the immense detail the British Government went into in anticipation of Nixon's visit.

as well as IAF bombardment of other Egyptian targets.

May 1969
Vietnam: Nixon offers 8-point peace terms, proposing simultaneous withdrawal of forces.

25 Sudan: Army coup overthrows the government.

June 1969
Gibraltar: General Franco lays economic siege to the 'Rock'.
Vietnam: American troops start to be withdrawn under a 'Vietnamisation' programme.

August 1969
Ireland: Violence in Belfast and Londonderry.
Vietnam: Nixon starts troop withdrawals. Communist small scale offensive launched.

12 Ireland: Battle of the Bogside (Derry). The Orange Apprentice Boys of Londonderry hold a parade. Rioting breaks out and 1,000 police arrive to contain the crowd. Bogside marks a pivitol point where the troubles in Ireland move away from civil rights issues and toward religious and national identities.

14 Ireland: British troops sent in and are initially welcomed by Catholic minority.

29 Group commanded by Layla Khalid hijacks TWA plane flying to Tel Aviv.

30 Vietnam: US Army pulls out of the Mekong Delta.

September 1969
Ireland: British troops erect a peace wall between the Falls Road and the Shankhill Road in Belfast.

| Entebbe hostage rescue **1976** | Ogaden War begins **1977** | Mogadishu hijack ended by German special forces **1977** | Camp David accord **1978** | Russo-Afghan War **1979** | Vietnam-Cambodian War **1979** |

US soldiers, assisted by fighter helicopters, search for hostile Viet Cong in Combat Area Zone D.

I Libya: Muammar Gadaffi overthrows King Idris.

3 Vietnam: Ho Chi Minh dies and is succeeded by Ton Duc Thang.

December 1969
Ireland: The Ulster Defence Regiment (UDR) is established(seven battalions, one for each county and one for Belfast).
28 Ireland: Birth of Provisionals—The IRA Provisional Army Council issues a statement which signals the split between the IRA. The Provisionals emerge.

1970
Libya: Colonel Gadaffi becomes premier.
Ireland: The violence escalates, British troop numbers increase; they are now using CS gas and rubber bullets against the crowds, especially in Belfast and Londonderry.

Vietnam: US and ARVN troops enter Cambodia. Bombing of North Vietnam resumed close to DMZ.

January 1970
11 Nigeria: The last Biafran airstrip disabled as federal troops launch their final assault.

12 Nigeria: Biafrans capitulate —Colonel Ojukwu flies into exile.

February 1970
Jordan: Yasser Arafat becomes head of the PLO.

March 1970
Cambodia: Fighting breaks out between the Viet Cong and the Cambodian Army. While

1970-1979

- Third Indo-Pakistan War **1971**
- Bloody Sunday in Northern Ireland **1972**
- Fourth Arab-Israeli War **1973**
- Turks invade Cyprus **1974**
- Angolan Civil War **1975**
- Pol Pot and Khmer Rouge take Cambodia **1975**

P.L.O. president Yasser Arafat during a press conference he held after the Arab Leaders Summit.

Prince Sihanouk is abroad. General Lon Nol takes over as premier.

S Vietnam: The Americans intensify their air campaign against Viet Cong targets, such as the Ho Chi Minh Trail, to compensate for the reduction of their ground forces.

April 1970

15 Cambodia: Gen Lon Nol requests help from the USA, Thailand and S Vietnam.

24 Cambodia: The Americans say that Cambodia has been the victim of 'foreign invasion' and later, with S Vietnam, attack three Viet Cong areas (Fish Hook, Parrot's Beak and the Bulge).

29 Cambodia: S Vietnam launches an attack on Parrot's Beak, while American forces attack Fish Hook. The Viet Cong begin withdrawing.

May 1970

4 USA: During anti-war demonstrations, four students are shot dead by the National Guard on the campus of Ohio State University.

11 Lebanon: Israeli troops raid PLO camps, due to their continuous raiding into Israel.

June 1970

Middle East: The US proposed cease-fire in the War of Attrition between Israel and Egypt is accepted in principle.

29 Cambodia: Last US troops leave.

July 1970

Israel-Egypt: War of Attrition ends following pressure from USA and USSR on both sides.

| Entebbe hostage rescue 1976 | Ogaden War begins 1977 | Mogadishu hijack ended by German special forces 1977 | Camp David accord 1978 | Russo-Afghan War 1979 | Vietnam-Cambodian War 1979 |

President of Egypt, Anwar El-Sadat who was made President in 1970.

August 1970
Jordan: Fighting breaks out between Palestinians and the Jordanian Army.

4 Israel: With terrorist raids from adjoining Arab states continuing, Israel refuses all requests to withdraw to its pre-Six Day War boundaries.

7 USSR: Soviet leaders sign a non-aggression pact with West Germany.

September 1970
Jordan: "Black September" King Hussein of Jordan moves against the growing power of the PLO. Palestinian guerillas flee Jordan and take up residence in Lebanon. Continued fighting between Palestinians and the Jordanian Army. Syrian tanks cross the border to support the PLO but are quickly defeated.

6 Europe: PFLP hijack Swissair, BOAC, PanAm and TWA flights and divert them to Jordan.

27 Jordan: Truce agreed; Hussein forced to recognise Yasser Arafat and the PLO, but they in turn move their bases to Lebannon.

28 Egypt: Nasser dies of a heart attack and is replaced by Anwar Sadat.

November 1970
13 Syria: General Hafez al-Assad seizes power.

December 1970
India: Awami League victory in Pakistan elections.
Vietnam: American ground forces down to 280,000 men.

1971
Uganda: Milton Obote is ousted by Colonel

1970-1979

Third Indo-Pakistan War **1971** · Bloody Sunday in Northern Ireland **1972** · Fourth Arab-Israeli War **1973** · Turks invade Cyprus **1974** · Angolan Civil War **1975** · Pol Pot and Khmer Rouge take Cambodia **1975**

This former airfield is now the internment camp for IRA detainees. The hutments now have central heating and other modern amenities. The camp is called Long Kesh.

Idi Amin who institutes a reign of terror, ruining the economy in the process.
Vietnam: President Nixon announces more US withdrawals.

January 1971
Lebanon: Israel mounts more revenge raids into Lebanon against PLO bases.

4 Egypt: Sadat admits that six Russian soldiers have been killed in an Israeli raid on a SAM site.

February 1971
6 Ireland: The first British soldier is killed in the province.

8 Laos: Vietnamese forces begin operations into Laos against the Ho Chi Minh Trail, however bad weather and stiff resistance soon halt the offensive.

March 1971
India: Riots in East Pakistan lead to martial law and reinforcement of the garrison from West Pakistan.
Middle East: War of Attrition cease-fire ends.

12 Laos: The Viet Cong launch a fierce counterattack and S Vietnamese forces withdraw.
25 Bangladesh (East Pakistan): A state of emergency is declared, as the Pakistani Army begins a repression of Bengalis, with thousands killed. The leaders of the Awarm League are arrested.

April 1971
14 Bangladesh: The Awarm League declares the independence of Bangladesh.

18 Middle East: Federation of Arab Republics is formed, comprising UAR, Libya and Syria.

1976	1977	1977	1978	1979	1979
Entebbe hostage rescue	Ogaden War begins	Mogadishu hijack ended by German special forces	Camp David accord	Russo-Afghan War	Vietnam-Cambodian War

July 1971
Vietnam: Dr Kissinger secretly visits Peking.

13 Jordan: The Jordanian Army renews its campaign against the PLO.

14 Ireland: Serious rioting in Londonderry.

15 Morocco: King Hassan thwarts an anti-monarchist coup.

August 1971
Ireland: The government invokes emergency powers including internment. Further extensive rioting follows, with 7,000 houses being burnt down in Belfast.

October 1971
Bangladesh: Pakistani border exchanges of fire with India increase.
Ireland: The IRA bombing campaign spreads to mainland Britain.

(Left) US Air Force Captain Wilmer N. Grubb is given first aid while being guarded by his captors.
(Above) A Viet Cong prisoner captured during Operation Double Eagle is brought to the collection point by US Marines.

Middle East: Egypt expels Russian military advisers and decides to plan war against Israel.

30 Bangladesh: Indian troops cross the border to silence Pakistani artillery.
31 UK: An IRA bomb damages the Post Office Tower.

November 1971
21 Bangladesh: Guerrillas, supported by Indian armour, begin a major offensive against Jessore.

23 India-Pakistan: A state of emergency is declared. Beginning of the Third Indo-Pakistan War.

1970-1979

- Third Indo-Pakistan War **1971**
- Bloody Sunday in Northern Ireland **1972**
- Fourth Arab-Israeli War **1973**
- Turks invade Cyprus **1974**
- Angolan Civil War **1975**
- Pol Pot and Khmer Rouge take Cambodia **1975**

Hirohito (1901-1989) was Emperor of Japan from 1926 until his death in 1989. He was regarded as a divine monarch by his people until Japan's defeat in the Second World War led to the creation of a constitutional monarchy.

December 1971

Ireland: Three more battalions raised for the Ulster Defence Regiment.

3/4 India: Pakistani air strikes on Indian airfields herald the start of all-out war, which has been simmering throughout the year as the guerrilla war intensifies. Indian army units invade Bengal and quickly defeat the Pakistanis, also overruning the Rann of Kutch.
16 India: Dacca falls. Army in East Pakistan surrenders. Bangladesh proclaimed.

17 India: Pakistan accepts a cease-fire.

31 Vietnam: By the year's end there are 140,000 US troops in Vietnam.

1972

January 1972

13 Ghana: Colonel Acheampong leads a military coup.

27 Ireland: Gun battles between the IRA and British soldiers along the border.
30 Ireland: 'Bloody Sunday'—13 Catholics are shot by Paras in Londonderry as the situation deteriorates. More than 400 people will die during the year, seven on the mainland.

February 1972
Middle East: Sadat visits Moscow.

March 1972
Vietnam: Major NVA offensive launched across and round DMZ. Nixon resumes full-scale bombing of the North.

Entebbe hostage rescue **1976** · Ogaden War begins **1977** · Mogadishu hijack ended by German special forces **1977** · Camp David accord **1978** · Russo-Afghan War **1979** · Vietnam-Cambodian War **1979**

30 Ireland: The British government imposes direct rule.

Vietnam: N Vietnamese troops invade S Vietnam across the 17th Parallel.

April 1972
9 Iraq: The Iraqi-Soviet Treaty of Friendship and Co-operation is signed.

29 Burundi: A Hutu guerrilla attack kills several thousand people but with some help from Zaire the army of the ruling Tutsi minority manages to defeat the rebels. Thousands are killed and many more flee over the border to Rwanda and Tanzania.

May 1972
Burundi: Hutu attacks are launched from their bases over the border, but are driven back, Burundi forces entering Tanzania in a process that will run till the end of the year.

President Nixon and US Security Advisor Henry Kissinger during a walk in the park of Castle Klesheim near Salzburg, Austria.

1 Vietnam: North Vietnamese forces capture Quangtri. Three other simultaneous communist offensives are launched in various provinces and there is also fighting in the Saigon area.
10 Vietnam: Martial law is proclaimed.

30 Israel: A terrorist attack kills 26 people at Tel Aviv airport.

June 1972
21 Israel: Reprisal raids on PLO bases in Lebanon capture a Syrian general and four colonels.

July 1972
21 Ireland: 20 bombs explode in Belfast without warning, killing eleven and wounding 120.

31 Ireland: There are now 21,000 British troops

1970-1979

Third Indo-Pakistan War **1971**
Bloody Sunday in Northern Ireland **1972**
Fourth Arab-Israeli War **1973**
Turks invade Cyprus **1974**
Angolan Civil War **1975**
Pol Pot and Khmer Rouge take Cambodia **1975**

An Egyptian prisoner-of-war sitting in front of victorious Israeli soldiers.

in the province; launch of Operation 'Motorman' to eradicate 'no-go areas'.

August 1972
Uganda: Idi Amin drives out the Asians.

11 Vietnam: The last US ground combat unit (3rd Bn, 21st Inf Regt) withdraws from Vietnam.

September 1972
Vietnam: S Vietnamese forces recapture Quangtri.
Ireland: A eleventh UDR battalion is raised.

5 Germany: Black September movement massacres Israeli Olympic team in Munich.

17 Uganda: A guerrilla force invades from Tanzania, in support of Milton Obote. It is expelled by the army, newly supplied with arms by Libya. The Organisation for African Union (OAU), manages to prevent a full-scale war and peace is restored by the end of the month.

October 1972
11 Madagascar (Malagasy Republic): After extensive rioting, pressure from the military forces resignation of President Tsiranana.

1973

January 1973
Rhodesia: The border with Zambia is closed in a bid to prevent further guerrilla attacks.

8 Vietnam: Peace talks begin again in Paris.

27 Vietnam: Cease-fire signed by the USA, N and S Vietnam and the Provisional Revolutionary Government of S Vietnam.

February 1973
Middle East: General Ismail, Egyptian Chief of Staff, visits Moscow.

Entebbe hostage rescue **1976** | Ogaden War begins **1977** | Mogadishu hijack ended by German special forces **1977** | Camp David accord **1978** | Russo-Afghan War **1979** | Vietnam-Cambodian War **1979**

A destroyed Soviet-made Syrian 57mm anti-aircraft gun and ZIL truck are abandoned on the Syrian lines on the Golan Heights, two weeks after the beginning of the Yom Kippur War.

March 1973

1 Sudan: The US Ambassador is killed by Black September terrorists in an attack on the embassy at Khartoum.

3 UK: IRA bombs explode in the city.
28 IIreland: An Eirean naval vessel intercepts a ship carrying Libyan arms to the IRA.

29 Vietnam: The last US troops leave Vietnam.

April 1973

India: Indian troops annex the independent Himalayan kingdom of Sikkim.

1 Vietnam: The last US POWs released.

16 Afghanistan: A military coup sets up a new republic.

May 1973

19 Ireland: Nine die in sectarian clashes.

June 1973

Ireland: Six are killed by a car bomb in Coleraine.

29 Chile: A revolt against President Allende is crushed with support from the military.

30 Cambodia: Communist guerrillas launch a major attack towards Phnom Penh.

July 1973

Ireland: Mass arrests by police and military on both sides of the border.

1970–1979

- Third Indo-Pakistan War **1971**
- Bloody Sunday in Northern Ireland **1972**
- Fourth Arab-Israeli War **1973**
- Turks invade Cyprus **1974**
- Angolan Civil War **1975**
- Pol Pot and Khmer Rouge take Cambodia **1975**

Israeli soldiers atop a US-made Super-Sherman tank on Syria's Golan Heights, a week after the beginning of the Yom Kippur War.

August 1973

12 Ireland: Rubber bullets used for the first time by the RUC.

September 1973

11 Chile: Allende and 2,000 others die during a military coup led by General Pinochet, assisted by the American CIA.

19 Jordan: King Hussein declares a general amnesty and releases PLO prisoners.

October 1973

6 Israel: Yom Kippur War. Egyptian forces attack across the Suez Canal and assault the Bar-Lev Line. Using hand-held ATGW they maul unsupported Israeli armoured counterattacks. However unwilling to leave the safety of their SAM missile umbrella, they do not advance into Sinai and initiative passes to the Israelis. At the same time Syria attacks on the Golan Heights and it takes the Israelis some very determined fighting to stabilise this front.

7 Middle East: Syrian forces overlook Lake Tiberias and capture Mount Hermon.

8 Middle East: Israel counterattacks Egyptian forces east of Suez Canal.

9 Middle East: Israel holds Syrian advance.

10 Middle East: Israeli counterattacks restore position on Golan Heights and contain Egyptian forces east of canal.

11 Middle East: Israeli forces advance into Syria.

14 Middle East: Egyptian Second Army's major attack fails.

Entebbe hostage rescue **1976** | Ogaden War begins **1977** | Mogadishu hijack ended by German special forces **1977** | Camp David accord **1978** | Russo-Afghan War **1979** | Vietnam-Cambodian War **1979**

The body of a Syrian soldier lies next to a soviet-made T-54 Syrian tank, near the Syrian lines on the Golan Heights.

15 Israel: Israeli paratroopers supported by tanks, re-cross the Suez Canal, fan out and attack Egyptian missile sites, etc.

19 Middle East: Israeli break-out west of Bitter Lakes.

21 Middle East: UN Security Council calls for cease-fire on October 22

22 Israel: With the Egyptian 3rd Army completely cut off, the first cease-fire is agreed.

24 Israel: With Israel poised on the brink of outright victory, a second cease-fire is agreed.

30 Europe: NATO and Warsaw Pact countries discuss mutual force reductions.

December 1973
17 Italy: Arab terrorists kill 30 people at Rome airport.

21 Switzerland: Middle East Peace Conference convened in Geneva. Jordan, Egypt, SU, US and Israel attend, with Syria refusing.

1974

Angola: Negotiations continue with guerrilla groups towards ending hostilities.
Middle East: PLO terrorist activities continue all year, with 'tit for tat' attacks by Israel on their camps and bases in the Lebanon. Agreement is reached between Israel and Egypt for withdrawal and limitation of forces in Sinai.

January 1974
1 Ireland: A new power sharing executive is inaugurated -including both Protestants and

1970-1979

- Third Indo-Pakistan War **1971**
- Bloody Sunday in Northern Ireland **1972**
- Fourth Arab-Israeli War **1973**
- Turks invade Cyprus **1974**
- Angolan Civil War **1975**
- Pol Pot and Khmer Rouge take Cambodia **1975**

Chilean Army troops fire on the La Moneda Palace in Santiago, during a coup led by Gen. Augusto Pinochet against President Salvador Allende, who died in the attack on the palace.

Catholics.

9 Cambodia: Troops launch an offensive against the Khmer Rouge.

18 Israel: A military separation agreement is signed with Egypt, though vehemently opposed by Syria. UN Emergency Force takes up positions in the buffer zones established in Sinai.

23 Egypt: Israeli troops begin to withdraw from the west bank of the Suez Canal.

February 1974

4 UK: 11 killed by an IRA bomb in Yorkshire.

8 Upper Volta: A military coup takes place.

11 Cambodia: Rebels shell capital Phnom Penh.

15 Iran: 70 die in border clashes with Iraq.

March 1974

Israel: Border clashes with Syria on the Golan Heights.
Iraq: Iraqi Kurdish guerrillas, assisted by Iranian, American and Israeli weapons and expertise, mount an escalating armed struggle against the central government.

April 1974

Israel: Continuing border clashes with Syria on the Golan Heights.
Vietnam: Talks between North and South are broken off.
Mozambique: After the Portuguese army revolt, negotiations are opened with FRELIMO (Front for the Liberation of Mozambique) guerrillas to end hostilities.

Entebbe hostage rescue **1976** | Ogaden War begins **1977** | Mogadishu hijack ended by German special forces **1977** | Camp David accord **1978** | Russo-Afghan War **1979** | Vietnam-Cambodian War **1979**

General Augusto Pinochet (L) poses with Chilean president Salvador in Santiago, shortly after Allende appointed him the head of the army, just three weeks before the Pinochet coup that killed him.

May 1974

10 Israel: Golda Meir resigns as PM following popular protest over the Yom Kippur War. Yitzhak Rabin, former Chief of Staff of IDF and ambassador to US replaces her.

11 Israel: Kiriat Shmona Massacre—IDF storms building to release Jewish hostages, but terrorists kill 19. Israel then makes reprisal raids in Southern Lebanon.

15 Niger: A military coup takes place.

25 Portugal: A coup by middle-ranking and junior officers, topples the authoritarian regime. A military junta led by General Spinola then takes power, who then begin negotiations with guerrilla groups in the three Portuguese African colonies (Angola, Portuguese Guinea and Mozambique). There are now nearly 150,000 Portuguese soldiers in the three territories.

15 Ireland: Sinn Fein legalized—The Northern Ireland (Emergency Provision) Act of 1973 is amended making the Ulster Volunteer Force and Sinn Fein legal organizations.
Israel: Ma'alot Massacre—PLO (PDFLP) gunmen capture a school in Israeli Ma'alot, demanding release of PLO prisoners. They eventually kill 25 and wound many others.

17 Ireland: A car bombs kill 23 in Dublin.

31 Israel: Truce signed with Syria over the Golan after mediation by Henry Kissinger of the USA.
Ireland: The power-sharing experiment collapses.

1970-1979

Third Indo-Pakistan War **1971** · Bloody Sunday in Northern Ireland **1972** · Fourth Arab-Israeli War **1973** · Turks invade Cyprus **1974** · Angolan Civil War **1975** · Pol Pot and Khmer Rouge take Cambodia **1975**

The US President Richard Nixon (left) with Prime Minister Harold Wilson at 10 Downing Street.

June 1974
Palestine: Twelfth Palestine National Council resolves that the PLO will use all means necessary to achieves its aims.

July 1974
15 Cyprus: Archbishop Makarios overthrown by a coup backed by the military government of mainland Greece.

20 Cyprus: War begins as Turkish forces invade the island.

22 Cyprus: Cease-fire arranged.

23 Greece: Having backed the coup in Cyprus and tried to order war on Turkey, the military junta of the colonels falls.

24 Cyprus: Cease-fire breaks down. The Turks occupy half the island before a new cease-fire. Makarios returns, but the island remains divided, with the UN policing the cease-fire line.

August 1974
9 USA: Nixon resigns over Watergate and is replaced by Vice-President Gerald Ford.

September 1974
7 Aegean: Palestinian terrorists blow up a US airliner over the Aegean Sea.

12 Ethiopia: Haile Selassie deposed by a coup, with Col Mengistu emerging as the dominant figure, but not having countrywide support.

20 Mozambique: A transitional government headed by FRELIMO takes office, but racial violence ensues.

October 1974
5 UK: An IRA bomb kills five people in a

| Entebbe hostage rescue 1976 | Ogaden War begins 1977 | Mogadishu hijack ended by German special forces 1977 | Camp David accord 1978 | Russo-Afghan War 1979 | Vietnam-Cambodian War 1979 |

Guildford pub.

(Left) Ethiopian Emperor Haile Selassie I in Addis Ababa, a few months before he was deposed
(Above) Emperor Haile Selassie I on his coronation.

16 Ireland: riots in the Maze Prison, Belfast, and IRA bomb explosions in London.

29 Morocco: —Arab League Rabat Summit — declares that the PLO is the only legitimate representative of the Palestinian people. This makes it more difficult for Israel to conclude a peace treaty with Jordan on the basis of return of the West Bank, for Hussein declares that he is no longer empowered to act for the Palestinians.

December 1974
S Vietnam: The Communists launch a series of heavy attacks in the Mekong Delta and Phuoc Long province.
3 UK: The government pledges to cut defence spending by £4,700 million over the next ten years and reduce British forces east of Suez.

11 Rhodesia: A cease-fire to the guerrilla war is agreed.

November 1974
13 USA: Arafat speaks at UN General Assembly debate on Palestine with his pistol showing. UNGA recognises Palestinians right to sovereignty.

22 UK: IRA bombs kill 21 people in Birmingham.

1975
Chad: A military coup brings General Felix Mallourn to power. His regime is opposed by the Libyan-backed Chadian National Liberation Front (FROLINAT). Thus civil war begins.

1970-1979

- Third Indo-Pakistan War **1971**
- Bloody Sunday in Northern Ireland **1972**
- Fourth Arab-Israeli War **1973**
- Turks invade Cyprus **1974**
- Angolan Civil War **1975**
- Pol Pot and Khmer Rouge take Cambodia **1975**

A Northern Vietnamese communist tank driving through the main gate of the presidential palace as the city fell into the hands of communist troops.

January 1975

15 Angola: Civil War. An agreement for independence signed in Portugal turns the fight into civil struggle between three groups: the Marxist MPLA (Popular Movement for the Liberation of Angola) with links to Cuba, the FNLA (National Front for the Liberation of Angola) backed by Zaire and a UNITA (National Union for the Total independence of Angola) breakaway group.

16 Ireland: The IRA bombing and murder campaign is resumed.

29 UK: IRA bombs explode in London and Manchester.

February 1975

13 Cyprus: Turkish Cypriots declare a separate state for their part of the island.

March 1975

Vietnam: NVA launch offensive in Central Highlands. Thieu orders withdrawal.

5 Israel: A PLO attack on a hotel in Tel Aviv kills 11.
30 Vietnam: Da Nang falls to the Viet Minh.

31 Angola: Civil war begins in earnest.
Iraq: the Iraqi army launches another general assault on the Kurds.

April 1975

5 Formosa (Taiwan): General Chiang Kai-shek dies.

13 Lebanon: The Civil war begins after a massacre of Palestinians by the Phalange (a Christian and Maronite militia).

Entebbe hostage rescue **1976** · Ogaden War begins **1977** · Mogadishu hijack ended by German special forces **1977** · Camp David accord **1978** · Russo-Afghan War **1979** · Vietnam-Cambodian War **1979**

17 Cambodia: The Khmer Rouge take over the country, capturing Phnom Penh. The Pol Pot regime then goes on to bring death and destruction on an unprecedented scale.

25 Saudi Arabia: King Feisal is assassinated.

29 Vietnam: Saigon Falls.
30 Vietnam: S Vietnam surrenders to N Vietnamese forces and the US embassy is evacuated.

June 1975
4 Israel: A PLO bomb in Jerusalem kills 14.

25 Mozambique: The country gains independence.

July 1975
29 Nigeria: General Gowon is ousted in a military coup.

Vietnamese soldiers sitting on top of a tank posted in front of the presidential palace of the US-backed regime as hundreds of Saigon residents gather around after the city fell to communist troops

August 1975
15 Bangladesh: President Mujibur Rahman (the 'Father of Bangladesh') is killed during a military coup.
20 East Timor: The civil war begins.

September 1975
15 Lebannon: The capital Beirut is the scene of vicious internecine street fighting.

October 1975
Ireland: Protestant revenge killings escalate.

1 Angola: A large contingent of Cubans arrive; the Chinese supply UNITA; the USSR the MPLA.

November 1975
UN: UN Resolution 3379 equates Zionism

1970-1979

- Third Indo-Pakistan War **1971**
- Bloody Sunday in Northern Ireland **1972**
- Fourth Arab-Israeli War **1973**
- Turks invade Cyprus **1974**
- Angolan Civil War **1975**
- Pol Pot and Khmer Rouge take Cambodia **1975**

A Harrier's downward thrust raises a filmy curtain of spray as the Hawker Siddeley jump jet comes in to land on the 12,000 ton assault ship HMS Fearless.

with racism.

6 Morocco: The Green March (350,000 unarmed participants) invades the Western Sahara. Spain relinquish its desert colony.

22 Spain: A constitutional monarchy is installed following the death of General Franco.

December 1975

3 Laos: The Pathet Lao take over and declare a 'People's Republic'.

5 Ireland: End of internment during which nearly 2,000 were detained without a proper trial.

7 East Timor: Indonesian forces invade.
Angola: 40,000 people are dead and a million homeless so far in the conflict.

1976

January 1976

Angola: The Cuban-backed MPLA have successes against the anti-Marxist UNITA forces.

4 Ireland: 15 die in 'tit for tat' killings between Catholics and Protestants.

February 1976

3 Mozambique: President Machel puts the country on a war footing and seizes Rhodesian assets.

11 Angola: The OAU recognises the MPLA government and later Angola is accepted into the UN. However FNLA and UNITA guerrillas continue to operate. Cuban forces remain.

March 1976

Ireland: The British begin phasing out Special

| Entebbe hostage rescue 1976 | Ogaden War begins 1977 | Mogadishu hijack ended by German special forces 1977 | Camp David accord 1978 | Russo-Afghan War 1979 | Vietnam-Cambodian War 1979 |

Birmingham, where 21 died and 159 others were injured in the terror bombings of two city centre pubs, the Mulberry Bush and the tavern in the town.

Category status. After this date, all prisoners convicted of terrorist acts are to be treated as ordinary criminals and locked in H-Block.

24 Argentina: A military coup overthrows Isabel Peron and installs a military junta.

31 Middle East: Syria is invited into Lebanon by Maronite Christians.

April 1976
20 Rhodesia: Ian Smith's illegal UDI government calls up white reservists to help deal with the guerrilla raids from Mozambique.

May 1976
31 Lebanon: Syrian troops cross the border.

June 1976
Angola: 13 white mercenaries are put on trial: four are shot, the rest receive long sentences.

9 Lebanon: Syrian troops join in the war, attacking Palestinians.

12 Uruguay: There is a military coup.

15 S Africa: Widespread violence is sparked off by riots in Soweto.
16 Lebanon: US Ambassador kidnapped and murdered in Beirut.

25 Uganda: Idi Amin declares himself president for life.

27 Uganda: PLO terrorists hijack an Air France airliner to Entebbe, demanding that Israel release 53 Palestinian prisoners.

July 1976
2 Sudan: Diplomatic relations with Libya are broken off after an attempted coup.

1970-1979

- Third Indo-Pakistan War **1971**
- Bloody Sunday in Northern Ireland **1972**
- Fourth Arab-Israeli War **1973**
- Turks invade Cyprus **1974**
- Angolan Civil War **1975**
- Pol Pot and Khmer Rouge take Cambodia **1975**

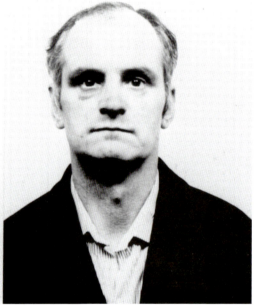

William Power (left), and Hugh Callaghan two Birmingham six.

Vietnam: A united Vietnam is declared a socialist republic.

5 Uganda: Israeli commandos rescue the passengers from the hijacked airliner at Entebbe in a brilliantly executed operation.

21 Ireland: British Ambassador to Eire is killed by an IRA mine.

August 1976
Mozambique: Hundreds are killed during Rhodesian army raids on guerrilla camps.

8 Ireland: the Women's peace movement is launched. During the year there are more than 7,000 terrorist-related incidents.

12 Lebanon: Christians capture the PLO camp, Tal al Zataar.

September 1976
Mozambique: Hundreds are killed during Rhodesian army raids on guerrilla camps.
Ireland: Kieran Nugent, Provisional IRA member, is the first prisoner convicted and not given Special Category status. He refuses to wear a uniform and wears a blanket to differentiate himself from the Ordinary Decent Criminals (ODCs).
9 China: Mao Tse-tung dies.

October 1976
Lebanon: A cease-fire —the 56th!—is arranged. It coincides with the Riyadh Peace Plan—which proposes a deterrent force and the withdrawal of Lebanese combatants. By now some 35,000 people have already died so far in this war.

6 Thailand: A violent coup follows civil unrest.

11 China: The 'Gang of Four' are arrested and

Entebbe hostage rescue **1976** | Ogaden War begins **1977** | Mogadishu hijack ended by German special forces **1977** | Camp David accord **1978** | Russo-Afghan War **1979** | Vietnam-Cambodian War **1979**

reforms initiated by Mao's successor Deng Xiaoping.

John Walker (left), and Robert Hunter, two of the Birmingham six Ulstermen charged with the murder of 21 people at the Birmingham pub bombings.

1977

January 1977
27 Europe: A European convention on the repression of terrorism is signed.

29 Britain: More IRA bombs on the mainland—seven explode in London.

February 1977
Ethiopia: Mengistu consolidates his hold on power.
Iraq: Anti-government riots by Iraqi Shias in Najaf and Karbala.

10 Rhodesia: Missionaries murdered by terrorists.

March 1977
8 Zaire: A small force of Angolans invade the province of Shaba (formerly Katanga). They are repulsed by some 1,500 Moroccan troops flown in by the French (financed by Saudi Arabia).
16 Lebanon: The Druze leader, Kamal Jemblatt, is assassinated.

18 Congo: President Mgoubi is assassinated.

May 1977
Ireland: British troop reinforcements arrive in anticipation of a Loyalist general strike.

June 1977
20 Israel: The right wing religious Likud party and Begin government take power. The Israeli

1970-1979

- Third Indo-Pakistan War **1971**
- Bloody Sunday in Northern Ireland **1972**
- Fourth Arab-Israeli War **1973**
- Turks invade Cyprus **1974**
- Angolan Civil War **1975**
- Pol Pot and Khmer Rouge take Cambodia **1975**

 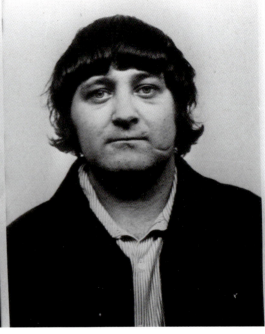

Noel McIlkenny (left), an Patrick Hill, two of the six Birmingham Ulstermen charged with the murder of 21 people at the Birmingham pub bombings.

settlement of the West Bank and Gaza is intensified following the rise of the extreme Likud party to power and influence in the government.

16 Sri Lanka: Tamil separatists riot.

July 1977

Libya: Egyptians mount a limited military operation after provocation by Libya.

3 Libya: Peace between Libya and Egypt—with PLO chairman, Yasser Arafat, plus other Arab leaders, acting as mediators.

5 Pakistan: A military coup overthrows the government and installs a repressive military regime under General Zia ul-Haq.

August 1977

8 Ethiopia: The Ogaden War begins when Somali guerrillas of the Western Somali Liberation Front, backed by army 'volunteers', invade in strength.

October 1977

13 Somalia: Palestinian and West German terrorists hijack an airliner and land at Mogadishu.

18 Mogadishu: German special forces rescue the hostages from the hijacked airliner

20 Thailand: The military re-impose control.

November 1977

Ethiopia: Somali forces cut the main transport link (the railway from Djibouti to Addis Ababa) and capture the strategic centre of Harar. However the Soviets, who have been supporting them with materiel, now switch their allegiance to Ethiopia, moving their 4,000 advisers over and stopping all military supplies. Cuban troops and

Entebbe hostage rescue **1976** — Ogaden War begins **1977** — Mogadishu hijack ended by German special forces **1977** — Camp David accord **1978** — Russo-Afghan War **1979** — Vietnam-Cambodian War **1979**

Egyptian President Anwar El Sadat, pictured at a press conference in Bonn, 1 April 1977.

weapons are then airlifted to Addis Ababa.

21 Israel: President Sadat of Egypt addresses the Knesset during a peace-making visit.

December 1977
5 Egypt: Sadat severs ties with Syria, Libya, Algeria and South Yemen who oppose his peace moves with Israel.
21 Egypt: Sadat meets Israeli Prime Minister Begin in Ismailia to continue peace talks.

1978
Cambodia: During the year numerous government troops are killed in border clashes with the Vietnamese.

January 1978
10 Iran: 50 die in anti-government riots.

23 Ethiopia: Ogaden War—fighting resumes between Ethiopians and Somalis.

February 1978
6 Chad: A cease-fire is announced by General Malloum. The rebel FROLINAT control much of the country, but have split into two factions.
7 Zambia: Rhodesian troops carry out raids into Zambian territory.

15 Ethiopia: Somalia sends regular forces to the Ogaden.

17 Ireland: An IRA bomb blows up a Belfast restaurant killing 20 people.

March 1978
Ethiopia: Somalia accepts defeat.

11 Israel: A terrorist attack on a civilian bus

1970-1979

- Third Indo-Pakistan War **1971**
- Bloody Sunday in Northern Ireland **1972**
- Fourth Arab-Israeli War **1973**
- Turks invade Cyprus **1974**
- Angolan Civil War **1975**
- Pol Pot and Khmer Rouge take Cambodia **1975**

"Carnival Against the Nazis" organised by the Anti-Nazi League and Rock Against Racism.

kills 30 people.

14 Israel: Israel invades Lebanon to deal with PLO terrorist bases.

18 Italy: The 'Red Brigade' terrorist organisation kidnaps ex-premier Aldo Moro.

21 Israel: Israeli withdraw from Lebanon.

31 Ethiopia: Somalia pulls troops from the Ogaden.

April 1978
27 Afghanistan: A violent coup organised by the Khalq ousts and murders President Daud Khan; its leaders (Nur Mohammed Taraki and Halizullah Amin) take over, with Soviet assistance.

May 1978
9 Italy: The Red Brigade murder Aldo Moro..

21 Zaire: French and Belgian paratroopers rescue 3,000 whites trapped in Kolwezi, after many killed by Katangese gendarmes.

June 1978
15 Kuwait: The PLO representative is murdered by the Abu Nidal group.
23 Rhodesia: More missionaries massacred.

24 N Yemen: President Ahmed al-Ghashmi is assassinated by a parcel bomb.

26 S Yemen: President Salim Rubai Ali assassinated.

July 1978
Lebanon: Heavy fighting between Syrian troops and Christian militiamen.

3 Vietnam: China cancels all aid and withdraws its advisers.

Entebbe hostage rescue **1976** — Ogaden War begins **1977** — Mogadishu hijack ended by German special forces **1977** — Camp David accord **1978** — Russo-Afghan War **1979** — Vietnam-Cambodian War **1979**

August 1978

2 Ireland: Cardinal O'Fiaich visits the Maze Prison and protests the unsanitary conditions. 300 Republican prisoners refuse to wear prison clothes and demand Special Category status. Protesters wear only blankets and smear the walls in their cells with their own excreta.

22 Nicaragua: The presidential palace is captured by Sandinista rebels.

September 1978

Nicaragua: Hundreds die in the anti-Samoza campaign.

8 Iran: The Shah proclaims martial law.

17 USA: President Carter announces the Camp David Accord concerning peace moves agreed between Israel and Egypt. However they are denounced by the Arab League.

Soviet leader Leonid Brezhnev (R) has to hold tight to his hat due to windy weather as he walks past the honour guard of the German army together with German Chancellor Helmut Schmidt.

20 Mozambique: Rhodesian forces launch attacks across the border to deal with guerrilla camps—killing more than 1,200.

October 1978

Iraq: The Shah of Iran is seriously threatened by a revolutionary movement guided by Ayatollah Ruhollah Khomeini living in exile in Najaf, Iraq. He is expelled by the Iraqi government.

30 Tanzania: Fighting with neighbouring Uganda is followed by Idi Amin's announcement that he will annex 710 square miles of Tanzania.

November 1978

6 Iran: The Shah imposes military rule.

1970-1979

- Third Indo-Pakistan War **1971**
- Bloody Sunday in Northern Ireland **1972**
- Fourth Arab-Israeli War **1973**
- Turks invade Cyprus **1974**
- Angolan Civil War **1975**
- Pol Pot and Khmer Rouge take Cambodia **1975**

The operational centre at RAF Fylingdales, Britain's early warning station perched atop the bleak Yorkshire moors.

December 1978

Iran: Millions demonstrate against the Shah and by the end of the month he has been deposed.

5 Afghanistan: USSR signs a treaty of co-operation.
15 Cambodia: The Vietnamese advance into Cambodia.

1979

January 1979

Cambodia: The Vietnamese Army attacks on a 200 mile front.
Chad: FROLINAT take control of 80 per cent of the country. The French Foreign Legion arrive to help halt the guerrilla offensive and a cease-fire is arranged but soon broken. The rebels are then pushed back.

8 Cambodia: Vietnamese take the capital Phnom Penh. Pol Pot and his supporters flee to the north of the country.

16 Iran: The Shah flees the country.
30 Iran: Ayatollah Khomeini returns from exile to a huge welcome.

February 1979

6 Congo. There is a coup in the capital Brazzaville.

11 Iran: An Islamic revolutionary regime headed by Ayatollah Khomeini assumes power in Iran.

17 Vietnam: Sino-Vietriamese War. Chinese forces invade Vietnam after provocation.

28 Iran: Clashes erupt between Khomeini supporters and Kurds.

Entebbe hostage rescue **1976** — Ogaden War begins **1977** — Mogadishu hijack ended by German special forces **1977** — Camp David accord **1978** — Russo-Afghan War **1979** — Vietnam-Cambodian War **1979**

Ayatollah Ruhollah Khomeini, 78, exiled leader of the Iranian Shi-ite Muslims, at prayers at his temporary refuge at Neauphle-le Chateau, 25 miles from Paris.

March 1979

3 Vietnam: China invades and captures the provincial capital of Lang Son. The Chinese declare that they do not want any Vietnamese territory, but merely a stable border.

4 Uganda: Tanzanian forces invade and smash the Idi Amin regime without much difficulty.

11 Uganda: Libyan troops arrive to help Amin.

13 Grenada: The government is overthrown while Prime Minister Sir Eric Gairy is abroad.

15 Iran: A cease-fire is declared between Kurds and Iranians.

17 Vietnam: Chinese troops withdraw after a warning from the USSR.

22 Ireland: IRA bomb kills the British Ambassador to the Netherlands.

26 Middle East: Peace treaty signed between Egypt and Israel.

30 UK: IRA bomb kills Airey Neave.

April 1979

Iran: Various prominent people, including the ex-prime minister, are executed.

11 Uganda: Kampala falls and Amin is deposed.

17 UK: Four policemen killed by the IRA's largest bomb yet—1,000 lb.

June 1979

Ghana: A coup is led by Flt Lt Jerry Rawlings.
Iraq: Anti-government riots by Shias in southern Iraqi cities and Baghdad.

1970-1979

Third Indo-Pakistan War **1971** · Bloody Sunday in Northern Ireland **1972** · Fourth Arab-Israeli War **1973** · Turks invade Cyprus **1974** · Angolan Civil War **1975** · Pol Pot and Khmer Rouge take Cambodia **1975**

6 Nicaragua: A state of siege declared.

July 1979

16 Iraq: Saddam Hussein assumes presidency, then purges the Baath Party. Leads to executions of senior party and state officials that continue into August.

17 Nicaragua: Sandinistas win after the US withdraw support for ruling faction; Samoza flees.

August 1979

Iran: More trouble between Kurds and Iranians. Iran cancels $10 billion US arms contracts.

3 Equatorial Guinea: The brutal dictator Francisco Nguema is overthrown.

22 Ireland: Lord Mountbatten, uncle of Queen Elizabeth II, is murdered along with three others when his boat is blown up by an IRA bomb at Mullaghmore, Co. Sligo.

(Left) Airey Neave at the Brighton Tory Conference. (Above) The mangled remains of the blue Vauxhall car belonging to Mr Airey Neave, after the car bomb.

27 Ireland: 18 British soldiers killed by IRA bomb—total of soldiers killed rises to 316 since 1969.

September 1979

Central African Republic: Emperor Bokassa is overthrown.

Equatorial Guinea: The dictator Francisco Nguema is executed.

October 1979

16 El Salvador: A military coup overthrows the dictator General Carlos Romero, in the hope of bringing democracy. Instead, civil war begins.

26 S Korea: President Park Chung Hee is assassinated.

Entebbe hostage rescue 1976　Ogaden War begins 1977　Mogadishu hijack ended by German special forces 1977　Camp David accord 1978　Russo-Afghan War 1979　Vietnam-Cambodian War 1979

30 Iraq: Iraq demands a revision of the 1975 border treaty with Iran.

The Prince of Wales Gives his speech at the service for Earl Mountbatten at Westminster Abbey.

November 1979
Chad: General Mallourn is deposed and flees to Nigeria. A provisional government is set up, but a power struggle soon develops between President Queddei and defence minister Habre.

Iran: Iranian students occupy US embassy in Tehran and seize documents and diplomats. Iran abrogates the March 1959 mutual military agreement with the US.

4 Iran: The US embassy in Tehran is besieged and 53 US citizens are taken hostage.

20 Saudi Arabia: Shi'ite fanatics capture the Great Mosque in Mecca.

24 Saudi Arabia: Saudi troops recapture the Great Mosque.

December 1979
Rhodesia (Zimbabwe): Ian Smith's UDI comes to an end at a conference in Britain in December and the British re-assume rule. But a deepening split between Mugabe's ZANU (Zimbabze National Union) and Nkomo's ZAPU (Zimbabwe African People's Union) parties bodes ill for the future.

1 Iran: Iranians approve the new constitution in a referendum

2 Iran: Ayatollah Khomeni becomes absolute ruler.

14 Iran: Tehran announces an Iraqi incursion into Iran which is repulsed

1980-1989

Sino-Vietnamese War **1980** · Iran-Iraq War **1980** · Iraq nuclear plant bombed **1981** · Falklands War **1982** · Israel invades Lebanon **1982** · US invades Grenada **1983**

Members of the Special Air Service (SAS) enter the Iranian Embassy May 5, 1980, to end a six day siege in Central London.

25 Afghanistan: Soviet forces invade with four motorised divisions; airborne troops seize Kabul airport, and special forces kill President Halizullah Amin.

31 Cambodia: The Vietnamese publish details of Khmer Rouge massacres—3,000,000 have died under the Pol Pot regime.

1980

January 1980

5 Iran-Iraq: Five-day Iranian counteroffensive in the Dezful-Susangard area begins.

10 Iran-Iraq: The Iranian counteroffensive ends in failure.

26 Iran: Abol Hassan Bani-Sadr is elected president of the Islamic of Iran.

31 Afghanistan: Russo-Afghan War. By the end of the month there are more than 80,000 Soviet troops in support of the Afghan Army and fierce fighting is taking place against the Mujahedin.

Israel: Israel agrees to allow a UN peace-keeping force into Sinai.

February 1980

Iran-Iraq: Border clashes against a background of hostile propaganda leads to war.

22 Afghanistan: Martial law is proclaimed after anti-Soviet riots in Kabul.

March 1980

Zimbabwe: ZANU wins the elections and Robert Mugabe is elected president.

April 1980

IRA bomb Grand Hotel Brighton aiming for Mrs Thatcher **1984** • State of emergency declared in South Africa **1985** • Removal of Russian troops from Afghanistan starts **1986** • The Intifada begins in Gaza **1987** • SAS kill IRA cell in Gibraltar **1988** • Berlin Wall comes down **1989**

1 Iraq: An unsuccessful attempt to assassinate Tariq Aziz, premier of Iraq.

8 Iraq: Ayatollah Muhammad an eminent leader of Iraqi Shias, is executed.

17 Iran: Ayatollah Khomeini urges the Iraqi people to overthrow the Baathist regime.

18 Zimbabwe: Britain's last African colony becomes independent.

25 Egypt: The last Israeli forces withdraw from Sinai.

30 UK: Terrorists seize the Iranian embassy.

May 1980
5 UK: Iranian embassy stormed by the SAS.

23 S Africa: Five white SA soldiers and 81 black nationalist guerrillas are killed in a border

(Left) A police negotiator, his arms held wide, walks away from the Iranian Embassy, Princes Gate, Kensington. (Above) Trevor Lock, hero of the Iranian Embassy siege, when receiving the Freedom of the City of London.

clash on the Angolan border.

25 Iran: An attempted rescue of the Tehran hostages by US special forces ends in failure due to helicopter breakdowns.

July 1980
9 Iran: A military coup by monarchist officers is thwarted.

August 1980
Afghanistan: Soviet/Kabul forces launch a new type of co-ordinated operations in the Sarobi valley in August, with some success.

5 Iraq: President Saddam visits Riyadh and consults monarch on his plans for war with Iran.

16 India: 150 die in sectarian violence in Uttar

1980-1989

Sino-Vietnamese War **1980** | Iran-Iraq War **1980** | Iraq nuclear plant bombed **1981** | Falklands War **1982** | Israel invades Lebanon **1982** | US invades Grenada **1983**

Three bodies after a bomb attack in Munich, Germany, 26 September 1980. A bomb exploded in a waste paper basket near the entrance of the world-famous festival 'Oktoberfest' killing 12 people and injuring hundreds.

Pradesh.

September 1980

4 Iraq: The Iranians shell Iraqi towns of Khanaqin and Mandali.

7 Turkey: There is a military coup.

14 Turkey: General Kenan Evren becomes president.

17 Iraq: Saddam Hussein abrogates the 1975 treaty and claims full sovereignty over the Shatt at Arab waterway.

20 Iran: Iran calls up military reservists

22 Iran-Iraq: The Iraqi army invades Iran simulateaneously in eight places, bombs Iranian airfields and military installations.

23 Iran-Iraq: Iran retaliates with air raids of her own.

October 1980

Chad: Libyan forces, supporting President Queddei, occupy the capital Ndjamena.

10 Iran-Iraq: Iraq captures Khorramshahr.

14 Iran-Iraq: The Iraqis begin to attack Susangard.
17 Iran-Iraq: The Iraqis fail to gain Susangard.

24 Middle East: Iraqis attack and destroy the Abadan oil refinery. The UN Security Council urges a cessation of hostilities but to no avail.

27 Ireland: First hunger strike—Tommy McKearney and six other IRA members

1984	1985	1986	1987	1988	1989
IRA bomb Grand Hotel Brighton aiming for Mrs Thatcher	State of emergency declared in South Africa	Removal of Russian troops from Afghanistan starts	The Intifada begins in Gaza	SAS kill IRA cell in Gibraltar	Berlin Wall comes down

General view of Bologna Central Train Station, in Italy, where a terrorist bomb blast killed 81 people.

demand the right to wear their own clothes.

November 1980
Iran-Iraq: Iranian begin a push to retake territory around Abadan and north of Susangard, which continues into December.
10 Middle East: Iraqis capture Khorramshahr, but fail to take Susangard.

December 1980
Chad: Libyan troops replaced by Organisation of African Unity (OAU) peace-keeping force.

10 Poland: NATO leaders warn the USSR to stay out of Polish affairs, following a concentration of troops on the border after Solidarity leader Lech Walesa's union success.

31 Afghanistan: Soviet/Kabul forces try to prevent rebel infiltration from Pakistan.

1981

January 1981
El Salvador: The military junta proclaim martial law.

Afghanistan: Heavy fighting in the Logar valley between the Mujahedin and government troops is followed by a highly successful guerrilla raid on the Soviet air base at Bagram. A joint Soviet-Afghan retaliatory 'expedition' ends in failure as the tribesmen merely melt away into the mountains.
Chad: During the year Libya's leader, Colonel Gadaffi, proclaims a union with Chad, but there is much opposition to it and Libyan troops are withdrawn.

10 Iran-Iraq: Iran's counteroffensive round

1980-1989

Sino-Vietnamese War **1980** | Iran-Iraq War **1980** | Iraq nuclear plant bombed **1981** | Falklands War **1982** | Israel invades Lebanon **1982** | US invades Grenada **1983**

Susangard proves unsuccessful

20 Iran: The US embassy hostages in Tehran are released.

25 China: The 'Gang of Four' are sentenced to life imprisonment.

February 1981

Zimbabwe: 300 people die in clashes between rival guerrilla groups. In March more deaths follow when government troops crush a rebellion by supporters of Joshua Nkomo.

9 Poland: General Jaruzelski takes over as prime minister.

23 Spain: Members of the Civil Guard, led by Colonel Molina, invade the parliament chamber as part of an attempted coup by troops under General Bosch. The plot collapses in 24 hours after King Carlos condemns it.

Another view of Bologna Central Train Station, after the terrorist bomb blast that decimated part of the station.

March 1981

1 Ireland: March Bobby Sands begins a hunger strike.

27 Poland: Solidarity independent trades union, led by Lech Walesa, calls for a national strike.

30 USA: President Reagan survives an assassination attempt in Washington, but is wounded.

April 1981

9 Ireland: Sands elected MP Forty days into his hunger strike, Sands wins the seat for Fermanagh-South Tyrone.

25 UK: An assassination attempt on the Israeli Ambassador in London.

IRA bomb Grand Hotel Brighton aiming for Mrs Thatcher **1984** | State of emergency declared in South Africa **1985** | Removal of Russian troops from Afghanistan starts **1986** | The Intifada begins in Gaza **1987** | SAS kill IRA cell in Gibraltar **1988** | Berlin Wall comes down **1989**

*Ronald Reagan, Governor of California. *05/06/04: Former US President Ronald Reagan has died a family friend said.*

May 1981

5 Ireland: Bobby Sands dies on 66th day of hunger strike leading to rioting in north and south: 100,000 attend his funeral. The next day provisional IRA prisoner, Joe McDonnell starts a hunger strike to take the place of Sands. Another nine IRA members will fast to death.

21 Iran: Khomeini dismisses Bani Sadr.

30 Bangladesh: President Ziaur Rahman is assassinated in an army coup led by General Manzur Ahmed.

June 1981

8 Iraq: Iraqi nuclear plant destroyed by Israeli aircraft.

10 Ireland: IRA terrorists shoot their way out of Crumlin Road Prison.

July 1981

Iran-Iraq: Iran mounts a small series of attacks around Abadan.

August 1981

30 Iran: The president and the prime minister are killed in a bomb blast.

September 1981

3 Poland: Soviet troops carry out manoeuvres near Polish border.

29 Iran-Iraq: The Iranians recapture Abadan

October 1981

1 Lebanon: A PLO centre is blown up in Beirut with 50 people killed.

1980-1989

Sino-Vietnamese War 1980 | Iran-Iraq War 1980 | Iraq nuclear plant bombed 1981 | Falklands War 1982 | Israel invades Lebanon 1982 | US invades Grenada 1983

British nuclear Submarine HMS Trafalgar at its launch.

6 Egypt: President Sadat is assassinated by Egyptian soldiers. Mubarak takes over.

November 1981
Iran-Iraq: Iran slowly retakes territories around Susangard and Abadan

14 Ireland: Unionist MP Robert Bradford is killed by the IRA.

December 1981
2 Seychelles: A group of mercenaries led by Colonel 'Mad Mike' Hoare is intercepted at the airport before they can mount a coup, but they escape to South Africa aboard a hijacked Air India jet.

15 Poland: Martial law is proclaimed.

20 Falklands: With British authorization to exploit his two-year contract, aboard the naval ice-breaker *Almirante Irizar* Argentine scrap dealer C. S. Davidoff visits South Georgia to inspect some purchases and plan the dismantling of the equipment of a former whaling station.

31 Ghana: Jerry Rawlings attempts another coup.

1982

January 1982
Afghanistan: Build-up of Soviet/Kabul forces continues until there are more than 100,000 but they are still unable to break the resistance continues to attack convoys and supply lines. The year opens with heavy fighting in Herat and the western provinces.

- IRA bomb Grand Hotel Brighton aiming for Mrs Thatcher **1984**
- State of emergency declared in South Africa **1985**
- Removal of Russian troops from Afghanistan starts **1986**
- The Intifada begins in Gaza **1987**
- SAS kill IRA cell in Gibraltar **1988**
- Berlin Wall comes down **1989**

British paratroopers man a machine gun in the San Carlos Bay area.

Iraq: Kurdish guerrillas sabotage the oil pipeline to Turkey, escalating their insurgency.
Spain: The government agrees to lift its twelve-year siege of Gibraltar and joins NATO.

31 Israel: Israel agrees to allow a UN peace-keeping force into Sinai.

February 1982
Uganda: Some 70 people are killed in a failed coup.

27 Falklands: In New York, Argentina and Britain reach an agreement to establish a permanent negotiation commission.

March 1982
Iran-Iraq: Iranians begin to expel the Iraqis from the Dezful-Shush area.

18. Falklands: Argentine workers land in the Leith station in South Georgia without British authorisation. Official confirmation of departure is given on March 22, but some men and equipment and a flag are left behind.

22 Falklands: Britain protests against a violation of British sovereignty, warning that if any further attempt is made to land in South Georgia without authorisation, the British government reserves the right to take whatever action might be necessary.

23 Guatemala: General Rios Montt replaces General Garcia in a coup organised by junior army officers, after many years of guerrilla warfare. He stops the 'death squads' but does little else.

24 Bangladesh: General Ershad seizes power in a coup.

1980-1989

Sino-Vietnamese War **1980** · Iran-Iraq War **1980** · Iraq nuclear plant bombed **1981** · Falklands War **1982** · Israel invades Lebanon **1982** · US invades Grenada **1983**

Hidden from view in one of the hangars of the carrier HMS Hermes is some of the might of the British naval task force sailing south for the Falkland Islands.

25 Nicaragua: Fearing a US-inspired attack by exiles, a state of emergency is declared, giving the Sandinista government wide powers.

26 Falklands: The Thatcher government sends the *Endurance* to expel the Argentines from the islands.

April 1982

Iraq: Kurdish insurgency within Iraq intensifies.

1 Falklands: Argentinian forces invade and capture the islands. They also seize South Georgia.

2 Falklands: UN backs British protests.

3 Falklands: Argentina takes South Georgia Island. UN Security Council passes Resolution 502 calling for the withdrawal of Argentine troops from the islands and the immediate cessation of hostilities. First RAF Transport Aircraft deploy to Ascension Island.

5 UK: A task force leaves for Falklands. Lord Carrington (defence secretary) resigns on the same day.

10 Syria: The pipeline carrying Iraqi oil to the Mediterranean is shut off.
Falklands: The US secretary of State, Alexander Haig, arrives in London to begin shuttle mediation. The EEC approves trade sanctions against Argentina. Haig in Buenos Aires for talks with the Junta.

12 Falklands: A British 200-mile war zone round the islands comes into force.

17 Falklands: Haig meets Argentines again, but returns to Washington after talks break down.

IRA bomb Grand Hotel Brighton aiming for Mrs Thatcher **1984** State of emergency declared in South Africa **1985** Removal of Russian troops from Afghanistan starts **1986** The Intifada begins in Gaza **1987** SAS kill IRA cell in Gibraltar **1988** Berlin Wall comes down **1989**

21 Lebanon: Israel attacks PLO bases.

23 Falklands: Foreign Office advises British nationals in Argentina to leave.

26 Falklands: Royal Marines recapture South Georgia. Argentine submarine *Santa Fe* attacked and disabled.

29 Israel: Israel completes return of Sinai to Egypt under the peace agreement, including the Yamit settlement.

30 Falklands: Haig's mission officially terminated. President Ronald Reagan declares US support for Britain and economic sanctions against Argentina. Total exclusion zone comes into effect.

May 1982
Iran-Iraq: Iran begins a major offensive in the south .

Royal Marines training with anti-tank weapons aboard HMS Hermes as she steams south to the Falkland Islands as part of the task force.

1 Falklands: Harriers and a Vulcan attack Port Stanley (Puerto Argentino) airfield. Three Argentine aircraft shot down.
4 Falklands: HMS *Sheffield* sinks after hit by an Exocet missile. Also a Harrier shot down.

5 Falklands: Peru drafts up a peace plan.

7 Falklands: UN enters peace negotiations

9 Falklands: Islands bombarded from sea and air. Two sea Harriers sink Argentine trawler *Narwal*.

10 Afghanistan: Soviet/Kabul forces mount a major offensive in the Panjsher area with some success, but sustain heavy casualties.

1980-1989

- Sino-Vietnamese War 1980
- Iran-Iraq War 1980
- Iraq nuclear plant bombed 1981
- Falklands War 1982
- Israel invades Lebanon 1982
- US invades Grenada 1983

11 Falklands: Argentine supply ship *Cabo de los Estados* sunk by HMS *Alacrity*.

12 UK: 5th Infantry Brigade leaves for the Falklands aboard QE2.

14 Falklands: Three Argentine Skyhawks shot down. Prime Minister Thatcher warns that peaceful settlement may not be possible. Special forces night raid on Pebble Island; 11 Argentine aircraft destroyed on the ground.

18 Falklands: A peace proposal presented by the United Nations Secretary General, Perez de Cuellar, is rejected by Britain.

20 Iran-Iraq: Anti government riots erupt in Shia majority southern cities.

21 Falklands: The first British troops land at San Carlos and establish a beach-head.

A Wessex helicopter hovers overhead as HMS Antelope, still burning fiercely, sinks in Ajax Bay. She was hit by Argentine air attack, and sank after an unexploded bomb went off during an attempt to defuse it.

22 Falklands: Consolidation day at the British bridgehead.

23 Falklands: HMS *Antelope* attacked and sinks after unexploded bomb detonates. Ten Argentine aircraft destroyed.

24 Iran-Iraq: Iran retakes Khorramshahr and drives the Iraqis back to the international border.

Falklands: Seven Argentine aircraft destroyed.

25 Afghanistan: Soviet and Afghan pull back to Rokka and Dash-eRavat.

Falklands: HMS *Coventry* lost and *Atlantic Conveyor* hit by an Exocet.

28 Falklands: The *Atlantic Conveyor* sinks.

IRA bomb Grand Hotel Brighton aiming for Mrs Thatcher **1984** State of emergency declared in South Africa **1985** Removal of Russian troops from Afghanistan starts **1986** The Intifada begins in Gaza **1987** SAS kill IRA cell in Gibraltar **1988** Berlin Wall comes down **1989**

Second battalion, Parachute Regiment, take Darwin and Goose Green. Death of Lt. Col. H Jones. More air-raids on Port Stanley.

29 Falklands: Warships and Harriers bombard Argentine positions: 250 Argentines killed, 1,400 captured; 17 British killed.
30 Falklands: Shelling continues as British troops advance: 45 Commando secure Douglas settlement; 3 Para recapture Teal Inlet.

31 Falklands: Mount Kent assaulted by British troops.

June 1982
Lebanon: Foundation of the Lebanese Shi'ite Hizbulla Islamist terror group.
Chad: In mid-year Habre's forces seize the capital Ndjadamena

1 Falklands: Britain repeats cease-fire terms.

(Left) Argentinian soldiers captured at Goose Green are guarded by a Royal Marine.
(Above) The Union Flag and white ensign being raised on South Georgia after the island's recapture.

2 Falklands: British troops take Mount Kent.

3 UK: Attempted assassination of Israeli Ambassador Shlomo Argov in London apparently by Abu Nidal faction, backed by Iraq.
Middle East: Large scale bombings by Israel in Lebanon PLO send rocket northern Israeli towns.

4 Falklands: Britain vetoes Panamanian-Spanish cease-fire resolution in the UN.

5 Falklands: A British Infantry Brigade lands. Heavy fighting follows around Mount Tumbledown, Wireless Ridge and Mount Longdon; the Argentinians pull back to Stanley.

6 Israel: Israel invades S Lebanon—ostensibly

1980-1989

- Sino-Vietnamese War **1980**
- Iran-Iraq War **1980**
- Iraq nuclear plant bombed **1981**
- Falklands War **1982**
- Israel invades Lebanon **1982**
- US invades Grenada **1983**

A Royal Marine mortar team dug in and ready for action on the wet and windy slopes of Mount Kent, East Falklands.

to establish a fifteen-mile buffer zone. But they do not stop there and continue northwards.

8 Chad: Queddei is forced to flee.
Ireland: Argentine air attack on landing craft *Sir Galahad* and *Sir Tristam* at Bluff Cove; loss of 50 British troops.
9 Syria: Syrian Soviet SAM radar destroyed by Israel. Israeli-Syrian armoured engagements.

12 Ireland: British forces seize Mount Tumbledown.

14 Falklands: The Argentines surrender.

15 Iraq: Saddam Hussein says that Iraq's 'voluntary' withdrawal from Iran will be completed by the end of the month.

17 Argentina: General Galtieri's military junta is ousted after the fiasco of the Falklands War.

20 Falklands: Britain formally declares an end to hostilities, and the exclusion zone established around the islands during the war is replaced by a Falklands Protection Zone (FIPZ) of 150 miles.

29 USA: Discussions with USSR begin on START (Strategic Arms Limitation Talks).

July 1982
11 Iran-Iraq: failed assassination attempt on Saddam Hussein.

12 Falklands: Britain declares an end to hostilities and promises to repatriate POWs.

13 Iran-Iraq: Iranian forces invade Iraq, but their offensive to capture Basra fails.

IRA bomb Grand Hotel Brighton aiming for Mrs Thatcher **1984** | State of emergency declared in South Africa **1985** | Removal of Russian troops from Afghanistan starts **1986** | The Intifada begins in Gaza **1987** | SAS kill IRA cell in Gibraltar **1988** | Berlin Wall comes down **1989**

20 UK: IRA bombs kill military bandsmen in a London park.

August 1982

Afghanistan: Soviet/Kabul troops mount further offensives in the Panjsher area, inflicting substantial damage to the rebel infrastructure, but at the cost of the lives of hundreds of their own troops
Lebanon: Israel troops reach and attack W Beirut— heavy fighting with Syrians and Lebanese, and many casualties.

15 Poland: Following renewed government clamp downs, there are riots against martial law.

21 Lebanon: The PLO agree to evacuate Beirut under the protection of an international force—most electing to go to Syria.

22 Lebanon: PLO evacuation of Beirut—about

A ceasefire between British and Argentine forces on the Falkland Islands is agreed.

14,000 leave. New PLO headquarters in Tunis.

23 Lebanon: Bashir Jemayeel made President of Lebanon.

September 1982

14 Lebanon: Lebanese President-elect Bashir Gemayeel assassinated, by bomb operated by Habib Tanious Shartouni, apparently a Syrian agent.

15 Lebanon: Israeli invasion of West Beirut.

16 Lebanon: Christian Lebanese troops massacre hundreds in PLO refugee camps in W Beirut.

21 Lebanon: Amin Gemayeel, brother of assassinated Bashir Gemayeel, elected in his stead.

24 Israel: Peace Now movement holds record demonstration of over 300,000 people, demanding

1980-1989

Sino-Vietnamese War **1980** | Iran-Iraq War **1980** | Iraq nuclear plant bombed **1981** | Falklands War **1982** | Israel invades Lebanon **1982** | US invades Grenada **1983**

Bodies of Palestinians killed 17 September 1982 in the refugee camp of Sabra lying 18 September in the middle of a road as civil defense workers prepare to take them away..

end to war, and a commission of inquiry for Sabra and Shatilla PLO camp masscres.

29 Lebanon: US marines land to resume peace-keeping operations which were interrupted by the Israeli invasion.

October 1982

Iran-Iraq: Iranian attempts to capture Mandali fail.

8 Poland: After further rioting in Warsaw, the Solidarity independent trades union is banned.

November 1982

Iran-Iraq: Iran makes some gains in the disputed border area around Musian.

9 Afghanistan: Many Soviet/Kabul soldiers die in a fire in the Salang Pass tunnel, following a terrible road accident.
Lebanon: 90 US Marines killed by a suicide carbomber at the Israeli HQ in Tyre.

11 Ireland: The SDLP and Sinn Fein boycott the opening of the N Ireland Assembly.
Lebanon: Israeli military headquarters in Tyre destroyed in an explosion, killing 75 Israelis and 16 of their prisoners.

17 Iran: The Supreme Assembly of Islamic Revolution is formed in Tehran, with the aim of overthrowing the Baath regime in Baghdad.

December 1982

15 Spain: Spain reopens her border with Gibraltar.

1983

Morocco: Polisario forces attack Moroccans in

IRA bomb Grand Hotel Brighton aiming for Mrs Thatcher **1984** — *State of emergency declared in South Africa* **1985** — *Removal of Russian troops from Afghanistan starts* **1986** — *The Intifada begins in Gaza* **1987** — *SAS kill IRA cell in Gibraltar* **1988** — *Berlin Wall comes down* **1989**

the Western Sahara. January
Afghanistan: Early in the month the government's beleaguered mountain garrison of Khost loses its support base, allowing the Mujahedin to move closer to the city itself. In the Panjsher a cease-fire is agreed upon.
Lebanon: The multi-national peace-keeping force continues its activities, but the PLO and Shi'ites turn against it.

February 1983
India: More than 600 Muslim refugees are massacred in Assam.

7 Iran-Iraq: A major assault is launched over the border by six Iranian divisions, followed by as many as 200,000 fanatical Revolutionary Guards in the Fakeh region of Khuzestan, to capture the Basra-Baghdad road near Amara; however only limited gains are achieved.

8 Israel: Israeli Kahan commission find Ariel

*(Left) Bodies of Palestinians killed in the refugee camp of Sabra.
(Above) Israeli army Major-General Ariel Sharon during the Six Day War.*

Sharon and others indirectly responsible for allowing the massacre in Sabra and Shatilla Camps.
15 Lebanon: The Lebanese Army takes over control of East Beirut from the Christian militia.

18 Lebanon: A suicide car-bomber attacks the US embassy in Beirut.

March 1983
Iran-Iraq: Iraq attacks Iran's Gulf oilfields.

April 1983
10 Iran-Iraq: beginning of another Iranian offensive in the Ein Kosh area

11 Switzerland: UN peace talks concerning Afghanistan begin in Geneva.

1980-1989

Sino-Vietnamese War **1980** | Iran-Iraq War **1980** | Iraq nuclear plant bombed **1981** | Falklands War **1982** | Israel invades Lebanon **1982** | US invades Grenada **1983**

An Argentinian bomb explodes February on board the Royal Navy frigate HMS Antelope killing the bomb disposal engineer who was trying to defuse it.

14 Nicaragua: US President Reagan denies sending covert help to Contra rebels.

17 Iran-Iraq: Fin Kosh Iranian offensive fails.

18 Lebanon: Hizbulla hsuicide bomber destroyed the American Embassy in Beirut, killing over 60 people.

20–21 Iran-Iraq: Iraqis fire surface-to-surface missiles at Dezful.

25 Switzerland: Afghan peace talks break down.

May 1983
Nicaragua: Reagan admits to covertly aiding the Contras.
Lebanon: The Israelis withdraw from W Beirut and are replaced by the Lebanese Army, which is soon forced out by the PLO and Shi'ites. They are also defeated in southern Lebanon after the Israelis leave. US forces assist the Lebanese Army, bombarding Druse villages from the sea and bombing terrorist bases and Syrian missile sites.

20 S Africa: 17 people are killed by an ANC carbomb at the SA Air Force HQ.

June 1983
Switzerland: UN brokered Afghanistan peace talks resume.
Chile: Thousands demonstrate nationwide against General Pinochet's regime.
Chad: Queddei, with Libyan support, renews his rebellion and over the month gains control over most of the northern part of the country above the 18th Parallel.

IRA bomb Grand Hotel Brighton aiming for Mrs Thatcher **1984** State of emergency declared in South Africa **1985** Removal of Russian troops from Afghanistan starts **1986** The Intifada begins in Gaza **1987** SAS kill IRA cell in Gibraltar **1988** Berlin Wall comes down **1989**

24 Lebanon: Syria attacks PLO bases in Lebanon and expels Arafat.

30 Chad: The government forces recapture the Faya-Largeau oasis.

A Royal Navy sailor manning an anti-aircraft gun aboard HMS Hermes as the British Taskforce sails south to the Falkland Islands.

July 1983
Sri Lanka: 13 soldiers are killed by Tamil Tigers.
Iran-Iraq: Iran mounts offensives in Kurdistan and west of Mehran, with some limited gains.

21 Poland: Martial law is lifted.

23 Sri Lanka: Riots in Colombo fomented by the Sinhalese terrorist group SVP kill hundreds of people—mostly Tamils.

30 Iran-Iraq: the Iranians launch an offensive west of Mehran.

August 1983
Afghanistan: Mujahedin take the offensive around Khost and Urgun.
Chad: After bombing by Libyan aircraft Faya-Largeau oasis is retaken by Queddei's rebels. Later in the month French paras land to support Habre's forces and a cease-fire is arranged.

21 Philippines: Begino Aquino, chief opponent of the Marcos regime, is assassinated. Widespread anti-Marcos demonstrations follow.

31 Lebanon: UN troops are fired on and return fire.

September 1983
3 Israel: Israel begins partial withdrawal from Lebanon.

1980-1989

Sino-Vietnamese War **1980** — Iran-Iraq War **1980** — Iraq nuclear plant bombed **1981** — Falklands War **1982** — Israel invades Lebanon **1982** — US invades Grenada **1983**

Philippines President Ferdinand Marcos & Mrs Imelda Marcos. Imelda Marcos, the former first lady of the Philippines, was behind a plot to assassinate her husband's mistress if she refused to keep quiet.

26 Lebanon: A general cease-fire is agreed.

October 1983

18 Grenada: A revolt overthrows the government and the PM is murdered. The USA is asked to intervene by neighbouring governments.
20 Iran-Iraq: Iran makes gains in Kurdistan, near Panjwin.

23 Lebanon: A massive suicide car-bomb attack on residential quarters of US marines (UN peace-keeping force) in Beirut kills 241 marines. Simultaneously 58 French (UN) soldiers are killed by a similar car bomb at their barracks.

25 Grenada: US invade: the rebels are crushed within two days.

November 1983

Afghanistan: The Soviets begin a number of regiment-sized attacks in the Shomali area, but otherwise there are no major government offensives. Khost and Urgun remain besieged throughout the year.
4 Lebanon: 40 Israeli soldiers are killed by a suicide attack in Tyre.

December 1983

10 Argentina: Military rule comes to an end.

17 UK: In London an IRA bomb explodes at Harrods, killing five people.

21 Lebanon: Another suicide bomber kills 15 French soldiers.

1984

January 1984

Chad: French and Libyan troops are withdrawn,

IRA bomb Grand Hotel Brighton aiming for Mrs Thatcher **1984**	State of emergency declared in South Africa **1985**	Removal of Russian troops from Afghanistan starts **1986**	The Intifada begins in Gaza **1987**	SAS kill IRA cell in Gibraltar **1988**	Berlin Wall comes down **1989**

Maze Prison near Belfast, Northern Ireland, terrorists are isolated from each other by use o fthe "H Block" building design.

although some Libyan forces remain in the Aouzou Strip along the Chad-Libyan border.
Nigeria: General Mohammed Buhari becomes the new leader in a bloodless coup.
Lebanon: Syria refuses to withdraw her troops while US and other troops remain.
Ireland: The troubles continue with more IRA bombs.

3 Tunisia: A state of emergency follows food riots, which many think are instigated by Muslim fundamentalists.

22 Afghanistan: The siege of Urgun ends.

February 1984
Nigeria: Hundreds die in religious riots in the north.
Iran-Iraq: The Iranians shell Basra, Khanaqin and Mandali; the Iraqis fire surface-to-surface missiles at Dezful.
Lebanon: Shi'ite and Druse militia gain con-

trol in W Beirut.
7 Lebanon: troops of the multi-national force begin to withdraw because of the dangerous situation

16 Angola: Agreement with South Africa for withdrawal of its troops.

22 Iran-Iraq: the Iranians mount Operation 'Khaibar' in the Haur al Hawizeh marshes.

26 Lebanon: The last US marines leave Beirut.

March 1984
Afghanistan: In March the cease-fire in the Panjsher ends and the Mujahedin resume their

1980-1989

Sino-Vietnamese War **1980** · Iran-Iraq War **1980** · Iraq nuclear plant bombed **1981** · Falklands War **1982** · Israel invades Lebanon **1982** · US invades Grenada **1983**

Libyan Leader Colonel M. El. Gaddafi

attacks on convoys.

1 Angola: Withdrawal of S African troops begins.

16 Mozambique: An agreement is reached with S Africa to stop cross-border raids.
Iran-Iraq: The Iranians win control of Iraq's oil-rich Majnoon Islands in the marshlands.

21 Iran-Iraq: Chemical experts conclude that chemical weapons have been used against Iran.

27 Iran-Iraq: First Iraqi attack on Iranian shipping using French planes and missiles

April 1984
Iran-Iraq: Iraq escalates the tanker war in the Gulf.
Afghanistan: Operation 'Panjsher 7'. The Soviets begin to employ more heliborne commando raids against guerrilla bases.

3 Guinea: A military take-over follows the death of President Sekou Toure.

May 1984
13 Iran-Iraq: Iran retaliates by attacking shipping serving Saudi and Kuwaiti ports.

June 1984
2 India: The Indian Army launches an offensive against Sikhs who are seeking autonomy in the Punjab.

5 Iran-Iraq: Saudi Arabia shoots down an Iranian plane for airspace violation.

6 India: Indian troops, including tanks and artillery, storm the Sikh Golden Temple at Amritsar.

IRA bomb Grand Hotel Brighton aiming for Mrs Thatcher **1984** — State of emergency declared in South Africa **1985** — Removal of Russian troops from Afghanistan starts **1986** — The Intifada begins in Gaza **1987** — SAS kill IRA cell in Gibraltar **1988** — Berlin Wall comes down **1989**

The Cenotaph at Enniskillen with the devastated community centre in the background. 11 people died and more than 50 were injured in a massive IRA bomb explosion just before a Remembrance Day ceremony took place.

10 India: Sikh soldiers in the Indian Army mutiny.

12 India: June a UN-sponsored cease-fire on attacks against population centres takes effect, UN observers being posted at Baghdad and Tehran.

August 1984

Afghanistan: At the capital Kabul there is an increased use by the guerrillas of indiscriminate attacks using unguided rockets. The siege of Ali Khel in Paktia province is broken and the Soviets mount a series of operations in the east. There is also heavy fighting around Qala in the Hazara mountains.

September 1984

Ireland: An IRA arms shipment is seized.

20 Lebanon: Hizbulla hsuicide bomber destroys the rebuilt American Embassy in Beirut, killing 25.

30 S Africa: Many people are killed in continuing township riots.

October 1984

12 Ireland: A bomb aimed at PM Thatcher and the Cabinet explodes at a the Grand Hotel, Brighton.

16 Iran-Iraq: The Iranians recapture part of their disputed border territory lost to Iraq just before the war began.

30 India: Prime Minister Indira Gandhi is assassinated by two Sikh members of her bodyguard. Her death is followed by anti-Sikh riots; more than 2,000 people lose their lives.

1980–1989

Sino-Vietnamese War **1980** · Iran-Iraq War **1980** · Iraq nuclear plant bombed **1981** · Falklands War **1982** · Israel invades Lebanon **1982** · US invades Grenada **1983**

The shattered top four floors of Grand Hotel, Brighton, which was devastated by an IRA bomb that left five people dead and 31 injured during the 1984 Conservative Party Conference.

December 1984

4 Sri Lanka: Hundreds die in communal violence.

31 Afghanistan: Soviet losses are higher than in any other year.
Iran-Iraq: Shipping attacks for the year: Iraq 53—Iran 18.

1985

January 1985

Afghanistan: The Soviet/Kabul forces begin a series of search and destroy operations in the centre and east of the country. Kabul remains vulnerable to rocket, mortar and bomb attacks, although it is sealed from major rebel attacks and various operations are mounted to deal with guerrilla bases around the city.
Lebanon: The civil war goes on as Israel continues to withdraw from everywhere apart from a small southern strip, leaving Christian forces to fight it out with various Muslim groups in areas such as Sidon.

8 Cambodia: The Vietnamese launch a major attack, causing thousands to flee into Thailand.
15 Brazil: Military rule ends after 23 years.

March 1985

Iran-Iraq: The 'War of the Cities' begins again. Iran mounts an offensive in the Haur al Hawizeh marshes to seize the Basra-Baghdad road.

5 Iran-Iraq: Iraq bombs Ahvaz and Bushahr. Iran missiles Baghdad and shell Iraqi border towns.

8 Lebanon: Many people are killed in another

IRA bomb Grand Hotel Brighton aiming for Mrs Thatcher **1984** — State of emergency declared in South Africa **1985** — Removal of Russian troops from Afghanistan starts **1986** — The Intifada begins in Gaza **1987** — SAS kill IRA cell in Gibraltar **1988** — Berlin Wall comes down **1989**

Prime Minister Margaret Thatcher and her bespectacled husband Denis, leaving the Royal Sussex County Hospital in Brighton after visiting the victims of the IRA bomb explosion.

bomb blast in W Beirut, outside the Shi'ite Hezbollah HQ.

12 Switzerland: the START talks re-open in Geneva

17 Iran-Iraq: Iranian reach the Basra-Baghdad road—but cannot withstand Iraqi counterattacks and are driven back to their base. Both sides claim victory in this largest battle of the war to date.

31 Iran-Iraq: Iraq claims to have hit 30 Iranian tankers in the last three months.

April 1985

Afghanistan: Operations are mounted against the Maidan valley, SW of Kabul, with some success.

5 Sudan: General Nimeiry is removed from office by a military coup while he is abroad.

6 Iran-Iraq: A War of the Cities cease-fire is brokered.

25 Kuwait: Attempted assassination of the Kuwaiti premier.
26 Iran-Iraq: Iraq breaks the cease-fire and resumes War of the Cities..

May 1985

Lebanon: The Shi'ites launch more attacks on the PLO camps at Shaba and Chatila.
Sri Lanka: 150 deaths in communal fighting.

1 Nicaragua: The USA imposes a total economic embargo.

15 Afghanistan: Soviet-Kabul forces launch another campaign in the Kunar valley, tem-

1980-1989

Sino-Vietnamese War **1980** · Iran-Iraq War **1980** · Iraq nuclear plant bombed **1981** · Falklands War **1982** · Israel invades Lebanon **1982** · US invades Grenada **1983**

Defence Secretary Michael Heseltine MP, wearing protective hat and combat jacket, outside a quick reaction alert silo.

porarily relieving Barikot.

June 1985

Israel: Israel Unity government, headed by Shimon Peres, orders withdrawal from most of the conquered Lebanese territories.

15 Afghanistan: The Mujahedin capture Pechgur in the Panjsher after a night attack, taking many prisoners, which leads to another punitive raid—Operation 'Panjsher 9'. This succeeds in recapturing Pechgur, but all the prisoners are all killed. In the east, Khost is again under siege, however the garrison, reinforced from Kabul by air, holds out.

July 1985

20 S Africa: President Botha declares a state of emergency to counter the violence which has already claimed more than 1,200 lives.

27 Uganda: A bloodless coup ousts Milton Obote.

August 1985

14 Iran-Iraq: Iraq targets intense air strikes against Kharg island over the next two weeks.
21 Afghanistan: Soviet-Kabul forces launch a major new eastern offensive, with attacks around Bagrame, followed by a major heliborne operation in the Logar area.

September 1985

Afghanistan: A task force narrowly fails to take the guerrilla base at Zhawar near the Pakistan border.

8 Iran-Iraq: Iranians attack with modest success in the Rawandoz area of Kurdistan.

IRA bomb Grand Hotel Brighton aiming for Mrs Thatcher **1984** State of emergency declared in South Africa **1985** Removal of Russian troops from Afghanistan starts **1986** The Intifada begins in Gaza **1987** SAS kill IRA cell in Gibraltar **1988** Berlin Wall comes down **1989**

T-2 Blue Impulse training planes, 1980.

11 Iran-Iraq: Iranian attempt to assault Basrah halted by fierce Iraqi counterattacks.

13 Iran-Iraq: Iran trades American hostages for 500+ TOW missiles with the Reagan adminsitration.

November 1985
15 UK: Anglo-Irish Agreement This agreement is signed by PM Margaret Thatcher and Taoiseach Garret FitzGerald. It establishes an Inter-Governmental Conference to deal with political matters, security, and legal matters and the promotion of cross-border cooperation.

December 1985
31 Iran-Iraq: By year's end Iraq has hit 33 ships in the Gulf, Iran 14.

1986

January 1986
Uganda: President Tito Okello is ousted in a coup mounted by Yoweri Museveni, backed by the National Resistance Army (NRA).

13 S Yemen: President Nasser el Hassam's bodyguard murder most of the S Yemeni cabinet (on his orders), but some escape and a violent civil war breaks out in Aden along tribal lines. Fighting lasts for two weeks, with some 13,000 casualties. Hassam is defeated and flees to Ethiopia.

17 Iran-Iraq: President Reagan authorises the CIA to buy 4,000 TOW missiles to sell to Iran via Israel.

20 Lesotho: A pro-South African coup puts General Justin Lekhanya into power.

1980-1989

Sino-Vietnamese War **1980** | Iran-Iraq War **1980** | Iraq nuclear plant bombed **1981** | Falklands War **1982** | Israel invades Lebanon **1982** | US invades Grenada **1983**

An F-15J Eagle fighter plane at the Gifu base in Gifu prefecture.

26 Uganda: NRA troops capture Kampala.

27 Uganda: Rebel troops capture Jinja.

29 Afghanistan: An attack on Herat successfully destroys a rebel base.
Uganda: Museveni is sworn in as new premier. Deaths in the continual violence since the deposition of Idi Amin have now reached five figures.

February 1986
Chad: In February and March Libyan forces in the Aouzou Strip mount several incursions southwards, which are repulsed by Chadian forces with French assistance.

6 Spain: Basque terrorists (ETA) assassinate a Spanish admiral,.

7 Haiti: President 'Baby Doc' Duvalier is deposed and flees into exile.

9 Iran-Iraq: For the rest of the month Iran mounts three offensives, the southernmost (in the Faw Peninsula of the Shatt al-Arab) being the most successful, although they also capture the area near Lake Darbandi Khan in the Suleimaniya region of Kurdistan.
24 Philippines: President Marcos's corrupt regime ends after discovery of election fixing. Mrs Corazan Aquino becomes president.
Iran-Iraq: 1,000 American TOW missiles delivered to Iran through Israel.

March 1986
Afghanistan: Throughout the month government units are concentrated in Paktia for another offensive against the rebel base at Zhawar. The Mujahedin also suffer heavy losses in the Fariab province near the Soviet border.

- IRA bomb Grand Hotel Brighton aiming for Mrs Thatcher **1984**
- State of emergency declared in South Africa **1985**
- Removal of Russian troops from Afghanistan starts **1986**
- The Intifada begins in Gaza **1987**
- SAS kill IRA cell in Gibraltar **1988**
- Berlin Wall comes down **1989**

Iran-Iraq: The Iraqis fail to recapture Faw in a counterattack.

17 Iran-Iraq: The Iraqis capture Mehran and offer to exchange it for Faw, but the offer is rejected by the Iranians.

23 Afghanistan: The Rebel base at Zhawar falls after very heavy fighting and many casualties on both sides.

24 Iran-Iraq: UN Security Council condemns Iraq for the use of chemical weapons.

April 1986
Iran-Iraq: Kurdish guerilla activity increasesagain within Iraq.

17 Lebanon: Two British hostages are murdered.

May 1986
Afghanistan: Major General Mohammed

Lieutenant Colonel Antonio Tejero (C) holds a hand gun, in the Congress during the second voting of Leopolgo Calvo Sotelo as president of the government.

Najibullah takes over as general secretary from Babrak Karmal, although the latter stays on in Kabul for several more months in a figurehead role as president.

S Africa: In May SA forces carry out anti-terrorist raids on Zambia, Botswana and

Zimbabwe: Thousands are evicted from their homes at the Crossroads squatter camp near Cape Town.

Iran-Iraq: As a result of continuous Iraqi air assaults on their oil production, Iran begins to import refined oil.

3 Sri Lanka: Tamil separatists destroy an airliner at Colombo airport.

17 Iran-Iraq: Iraq captures Mehran and offers to exchange it for the Fao. Iran refuses.

1980–1989

Sino-Vietnamese War 1980 · Iran-Iraq War 1980 · Iraq nuclear plant bombed 1981 · Falklands War 1982 · Israel invades Lebanon 1982 · US invades Grenada 1983

President Mikhail Gorbachev (left) and Russian Federation President Boris Yeltsin during the Congress of People's Deputies.

22 S Africa: White extremists, led by Terre Blanche, break up a meeting in the Transvaal.

June 1986
Sri Lanka: Tamil separatists kill 50 people in bomb attacks the following month.

12 S Africa: A state of emergency is declared, with many blacks detained without trial.
26 Peru: 'Shining Path' terrorists kill eight in an explosion on a train in Cuzco.

July 1986
Iran-Iraq: The Iranians retake Mehran.

14 Spain: Basque separatists kill eleven civil guards in Madrid.

31 Afghanistan: Gorbachev announces a limited withdrawal of Soviet forces. Throughout the summer there is fighting around Herat which goes against the rebels, giving the government forces confidence that they will be able to manage once the Soviets withdraw.

August 1986
12 Iran-Iraq: Iraq's airforce succesfully completes the long-range destruction of Iran's Sirri Island oil terminal. By end August it has also carried out 120 air sorties against Kharg Island.

September 1986
1 Iran-Iraq: Iran mounts a successful limited offensive in the Hajj Vmran region of Kurdistan.

3 Iran-Iraq: Tthe Iranians build a pontoon to attack across the Shatt al Arab waterway.

16 Iran-Iraq: Iraqi air attack on Iran's Lavan oil refinery.

IRA bomb Grand Hotel Brighton aiming for Mrs Thatcher **1984** | State of emergency declared in South Africa **1985** | Removal of Russian troops from Afghanistan starts **1986** | The Intifada begins in Gaza **1987** | SAS kill IRA cell in Gibraltar **1988** | Berlin Wall comes down **1989**

October 1986
Afghanistan: Kabul premier Najibullah announces a policy of national reconciliation, with a unilateral cease-fire and limited power-sharing, but it is rejected by the rebels.

10 Iran-Iraq: Kurdish guerillas destroy Iraqi oil piplines near Kirkuk.
25 Spain: Basque separatists murder the provincial governor and his family in San Sebastian.

November 1986
Iran-Iraq: The row about USA supplying Iran weapons.

26 Iran-Iraq: Iraq's most distant air raid yet on Larak Island oil terminal.

30 India: Sikh terrorists kill 25 Hindus on a train in the Punjab.

Soldiers on the alert in the Springfield Road area of Belfast after a lorry was set ablaze, on the 20th anniversary of the deployment of troops on Ulster's streets.

December 1986
31 Afghanistan: The year closes with the defection to the rebels of Abdul Rasool, chief militia commander in the province of Fariab, also taking large quantities of weapons and food with him.
Iran-Iraq: The successful Iranian ground actions and successful air attacks by Iraq on Iranian oil refineries make it an expensive year for both sides. The year ends with the Iranian offensive (Operation 'Karbala Four') against Basra, which fails. Iraqi strategy shifts from defence to attack; the army is expanded; their air power used much more aggressively. By the end of the year Iraq has attacked 66 ships in the Gulf and Iran 41.

1980-1989

Sino-Vietnamese War **1980** | Iran-Iraq War **1980** | Iraq nuclear plant bombed **1981** | Falklands War **1982** | Israel invades Lebanon **1982** | US invades Grenada **1983**

A B-52 leaves on a bombing mission to the Iraqi capital of Bagdhad from the UK.

1987

January 1987

Afghanistan: The year opens with operations in Fariab province which end with guerrilla leader Haq Berdi defecting to the regime.

6 Iran-Iraq: Iran launches a major offensive—'Karbala Five'—to capture Basra.

13 Iran-Iraq: Iran launches an attack in the central sector near Qasr-e-Shirin.

15 Afghanistan: The Kabul governent declares a cease-fire and founds the National Reconciliation Commission; there is little reaction from the rebels.

17 Iran-Iraq: For the next week Iraq launches missile attacks on Tehran and other Iranian cities. Iran retaliates in kind.

19 Iran-Iraq: Iran mounts two more offensives in the south, its forces getting to within seven miles of Basra.

20 Lebanon: Hostage negotiator Terry Waite is kidnapped in Beirut.

February 1987

Iran-Iraq: War of the Cities suspended at USSR's behest.

13 Lebanon: Shi'ite militiamen stop UN relief supplies reaching PLO camps in Beirut.

26 Iran-Iraq: Iranian operation against Basra ends.

March 1987

Chad: Chadian forces, using trucks mounting

140

IRA bomb Grand Hotel Brighton aiming for Mrs Thatcher **1984** — State of emergency declared in South Africa **1985** — Removal of Russian troops from Afghanistan starts **1986** — The Intifada begins in Gaza **1987** — SAS kill IRA cell in Gibraltar **1988** — Berlin Wall comes down **1989**

TOW and Milan anti-tank missiles, attack Libyans in the Aouzou Strip, forcing them to abandon their heavy equipment and withdraw.

4 Iran-Iraq: Iran's fresh Kurdistan offensive in the Hajj Umran region achieves limited gains.

April 1987
Iran-Iraq: In April the Iranians and their Kurdish allies take the strategic heights near Suleimaniya, also ground around Mawet and Qala Diza.
Lebanon: Syrian forces end the Shi'ite siege of Shatila camp.

3 Iran-Iraq: Iranians begin draining water barriers in the south and attack Basrah.

9 Iran-Iraq: An attempt to assassinate Saddam Hussein near Mosul fails.

27 Iran-Iraq: Iran penetrates the Iraqi Kurdish

A milan anti-tank missile being test-fired by members of the Staffordshire Regiment during night excersises at Fallingbostel, West Germany, as the 7th Armoured Brigade prepares for deployment to the Gulf.

region round Mawet and Qala Diza.

May 1987
Iran-Iraq: International shipping hit by mines in the Gulf.

4 Afghanistan: Babrak Karmal leaves for USSR.
6 Iran-Iraq: Iran fortifies Fari Island, turning it into a naval base.

8 Ireland: Eight IRA members of E Tyrone Brigade are killed during an attack by the SAS while bombing Loughhall RUC station.

14 Fiji: Military coup is led by Col Rabuka.

17 Iran-Iraq: Iraq hits American frigate USS *Stark*, killing 37.

1980-1989

Sino-Vietnamese War **1980** | Iran-Iraq War **1980** | Iraq nuclear plant bombed **1981** | Falklands War **1982** | Israel invades Lebanon **1982** | US invades Grenada **1983**

Multiple Launch Rocket System, firing in Saudi Desert, by 2nd Field Artillary, during the Gulf War.

20 Afghanistan: Battle for Jagi begins and is won by the rebels after three weeks' fighting.

21 Sri Lanka: 100 people are killed by a terrorist bomb in a Colombo bus station.

June 1987
Iran-Iraq: Iran gains more territory in Kurdistan round Suleimaniya.
19 Spain: An ETA bomb kills 19 people in Barcelona.

July 1987
20 Iran-Iraq: UN Security Council calls for a cease-fire, but it is declined by Iran unless the UN first identify and condemn the invader.

29 Sri Lanka: India sends a peace-keeping force to check the violence, especially the massacre of Tamils. It becomes more involved than anticipated, and the force increases to 65,000 but still fail to halt the violence.

August 1987
Afghanistan: The guerrillas mount Operation 'Avalanche' near Sarobi on the Kabul-Jalalabad highway.

September 1987
Chad: After further border skirmishes with Libya, a truce is agreed.
Tibet: There are sporadic anti-Chinese riots throughout the autumn.
Iran-Iraq: American and European warships and minehunters sent to the Gulf.

21 Gulf: US ships destroy an Iranian vessel caught laying mines.

October 1987
Afghanistan: Government operations in Logar province are renewed, while in the north

| IRA bomb Grand Hotel Brighton aiming for Mrs Thatcher **1984** | State of emergency declared in South Africa **1985** | Removal of Russian troops from Afghanistan starts **1986** | The Intifada begins in Gaza **1987** | SAS kill IRA cell in Gibraltar **1988** | Berlin Wall comes down **1989** |

the rebels under Ahmad Shah Massud stage a number of daring and successful operations.

6 Sri Lanka: After the suicide of 17 captured Tamil Tigers, 200 Sinhalese are massacred in revenge.

8 Iran-Iraq: US destroys three Iranioan patrol boats adter claims they attacked a US helicopter.
12 Sri Lanka: Heavy fighting between Indians and Tamils in Jaffna, which Indians eventually occupy after suffering some 500 casualties.

16 Iran-Iraq: An Iranian Silkworm missile hits a US flagged tanker in Kuwaiti waters. US warships destroy Iranian oil platforms in retaliation.

22 Iran-Iraq: Iran attacks Kuwait's Sea Island oil terminal.

30 Ireland: The French Navy intercepts a huge consignment of Libyan arms and ammunition, including surface-to-air missiles on board the

Australian members of the Commonwealth Ceasefire Monitoring Force at an airstrip near assembly point 'Charlie', at Elim, east of Salisbury.

Eksund. from Libya destined for the IRA..

November 1987
Afghanistan: Soviet forces mount Operation 'Highway' to relieve Khost,
8 UK: 11 people are killed by an IRA bomb at a Remembrance Day parade in Enniskillen.

December 1987
Israel: Riots on the occupied West Bank and in the Gaza Strip, as the Palestinians begin the Intifada (violent resistance to Israeli rule).
Iran-Iraq: Iran attacks in the Fakeh area north of Basrah.

8 Palestine: First Intifadeh—Stone-throwing Palestinian teens attack Israeli soldiers relentlessly.

1980-1989

Sino-Vietnamese War 1980 | Iran-Iraq War 1980 | Iraq nuclear plant bombed 1981 | Falklands War 1982 | Israel invades Lebanon 1982 | US invades Grenada 1983

A Palestinian woman throws stones at Israeli soldiers, during Intifada ('Palestinian uprising') fighting in the West Bank, in Bethlehem.

29 Afghanistan: Soviet forces relieve Khost—this is the last major operation of the Soviet 40th Army before its withdrawal.

31 Iran-Iraq: The year ends with the Iranians staging probing attacks in the Fakeh area north of Basra. During this year Iraq strikes 76 ships in the Gulf, and Iran 87.

1988

January 1988

Ethiopia: The continued struggle between government forces and guerrillas in both Tigre and Eritrea goes badly for the government, the Tigrean Peoples Liberation Front (TPLF) in particular posing a considerable threat.
Iran-Iraq: The year opens with a minor offensive by Iran near Mawet in Kurdistan.
Israel: There is more bloodshed in the Gaza Strip and the West Bank. Foundation of the Hamas Islamic Brotherhood advocating the destruction of Israel.

11 Ireland: SDLP leader John Hume and Sinn Fein President Gerry Adams begin discussions for an all-Ireland settlement.
17 Nicaragua: President Ortega offers to lift the state of emergency and agrees a cease-fire with the US-backed Contra rebels.

25 Israel: Jerusalem's turn for demonstrations.

February 1988

Afghanistan: Soviet-Kabul forces begin an offensive in Helmand province.

1 Israel: Israeli troops kill two Arab youths in rioting.

IRA bomb Grand Hotel Brighton aiming for Mrs Thatcher **1984** • State of emergency declared in South Africa **1985** • Removal of Russian troops from Afghanistan starts **1986** • The Intifada begins in Gaza **1987** • SAS kill IRA cell in Gibraltar **1988** • Berlin Wall comes down **1989**

27 Iran-Iraq: Iraq renews 'the War of the Cities', with an attack on Saqqez, northern Iran. Iran responds with a missile attack on Baghdad; the Iraqis respond with the first long range missile attack on Tehran.

A Palestinian man fires stones from his catapult at Israeli soldiers, during Intifada ('Palestinian uprising') fighting in the West Bank, in Bethlehem.

March 1988
Tibet: Chinese troops clamp down on anti-Chinese riots in Lhasa; over 500 arrests.
Iran-Iraq: Iranian offensive in Kurdistan.
Ireland: British SAS kill three IRA bombers in Gibraltar.

13 Iran-Iraq: Iran launches two offensives in Kurdistan.

15 Iran-Iraq: With the help of Kurdish allies Iran captures Halabja.

16 Ireland: A Loyalist gunman kills three at an IRA funeral.
Iran-Iraq: The Iraqi airforce chemically bombs Halabja, killing over 4000 people.

19 Ireland: A mob lynch two British soldiers at a Belfast funeral.
20 Israel: The first Israeli soldier is killed in the Intifada.

April 1988
Iran-Iraq: Continued Iranian offensive in Kurdistan.

14 Afghanistan: Afghanistan and Pakistan sign a treaty pledging non-interference and guaranteeing the withdrawal of Soviet forces—50 per cent by 15 August, the remainder by 15 May
Afghanistan: The Soviet withdrawal begins.
Ethiopia: An attempted coup by a group of dissident army officers takes place while

1980-1989

Sino-Vietnamese War 1980 · Iran-Iraq War 1980 · Iraq nuclear plant bombed 1981 · Falklands War 1982 · Israel invades Lebanon 1982 · US invades Grenada 1983

Masked gunmen fire shots over the coffin of IRA hunger striker Raymond McCreesh, draped in the Irish flag (foreground) in Camlough, South Armagh.

President Mengistu is out of the country.

16 Iran-Iraq: The Iraqis recapture the Faw Peninsula with the use of chemical weapons.

18 Iran-Iraq: Iraqi warships destroy two Iranian oil platforms, two Iranian frigates and a missile boat.

20 Iran-Iraq: Iraq ends the War of the Cities. It has fired over 200 missiles; Iran 77.

30 Sri Lanka: Tamil terrorist attacks kill 40 people.

May 1988

3 Israel: Israeli armoured force strikes at terrorists in southern Lebanon. The Intifada continues.

6 Ethiopia: After several days of heavy fighting in Addis Ababa the coup is defeated.

7 Lebanon: Particularly fierce fighting erupts between rival militias in Beirut. It ends when Syrian troops step in to end the fighting which kills 74 people in three days.

18 India: Sikh militants give up a 10-day occupation of the Golden Temple in Amritsar.

23 Iran-Iraq: The Iraqis mount assaults over the next two weeks in the northern, central and southern areas, again using chemical weapons. They take Shalamche, Mehran, the Majnoon islands, Mawet and other areas, using poison gas delivered by bombs and shells.

June 1988

Afghanistan: Over this month and the next Kabul is subjected to more than 120 heavy rocket attacks

1984	1985	1986	1987	1988	1989
IRA bomb Grand Hotel Brighton aiming for Mrs Thatcher	State of emergency declared in South Africa	Removal of Russian troops from Afghanistan starts	The Intifada begins in Gaza	SAS kill IRA cell in Gibraltar	Berlin Wall comes down

Vulcan- the world's first strategic bomber of delta-wing configuration, capable of carrying 21 bombs over a long range and attacking accurately at night or in any weather from low level.

18 Iran-Iraq: Both countries are by now war-weary, especially Iran which accepts the UN Security Council ruling to end hostilities, but refuses to deal direct with the Iraqis.

19–22 Iran-Iraq: Iraq captures Mehran using poison gas.

25 Iran-Iraq: Iraq recaptures the Majnoon Islands.

29 Afghanistan: 20,000 Soviet troops have left so far.

30 Iran-Iraq: Iraq retakes Mawet in Kurdistan.

July 1988

3 Burma: Martial law is proclaimed.
Iran-Iraq: US mistakenly shoots down an Iranian passenger plane, killing 300 people.

12 Iran-Iraq: Iraq regains the Musian border area.

22 Iran-Iraq: Iraq mounts further offensives in all sectors over the next week. These fail in the north but succeed elsewhere. Iran subsequently regains most of the lost ground.

August 1988

Afghanistan: More than 400 rockets have now been fired at Kabul this year, killing hundreds of people.

Burundi: A renewal of ethnic conflict leads to some 30,000 deaths.

Angola: A peace agreement is signed in Geneva by S Africa, Cuba and Angola. The civil war ends. S Africa agrees to stop helping anti-government guerrillas and to grant independence to Namibia where SWAPO guerrillas have been fighting for 25 years (the SWAPO leader, Sam Nujamo, becomes Namibia's first president). In return, Cuba agrees to withdraw

1980-1989

- Sino-Vietnamese War **1980**
- Iran-Iraq War **1980**
- Iraq nuclear plant bombed **1981**
- Falklands War **1982**
- Israel invades Lebanon **1982**
- US invades Grenada **1983**

Ms. Benazir Bhutto, the ex-prime minister of Pakistan. Bhutto accused Pakistan's President Pervez Musharraf of covering up a vast scandal involving the leaking of nuclear secrets to Libya, Iran and North Korea.

its 50,000 troops who have been propping up the Marxist regime in Angola.
Iran-Iraq: UN investigators conclude that Iraq has made extensive use of chemical weapons in the spring and summer.

8 Iran-Iraq: Iraq withdraws its demand for direct talks with Iran.
9 Afghanistan: The Mujahadin rebels capture Konduz.

17 Afghanistan: Soviet-Kabul forces recapture Konduz.
Pakistan: President General Zia, the American Ambassador and various pro-Mujahedin persons are killed in a mid-air explosion, thought to be the work of Pakistani fundamentalists opposed to the General's policies.

20 Iran-Iraq: A cease-fire finally comes into effect, bringing the eight-year war to an end.
Ireland: 6 British soldiers are killed in a bus on an Ulster road.

31 Ireland: A bungled IRA bomb kills two civilians.

September 1988

Afghanistan: The Kunar area falls to the Mujahadin rebels.
USSR: Anti-Armenian riots in the NagornoKarabakh area of Azerbaijan. Order has to be restored by Soviet troops.

18 Burma: General Saw Maung leads a military coup and then breaks up demonstrations in Rangoon with the loss of over 1,000 lives.

30 Pakistan: Hundreds killed in ethnic violence.

IRA bomb Grand Hotel Brighton aiming for Mrs Thatcher **1984** *State of emergency declared in South Africa* **1985** *Removal of Russian troops from Afghanistan starts* **1986** *The Intifada begins in Gaza* **1987** *SAS kill IRA cell in Gibraltar* **1988** *Berlin Wall comes down* **1989**

October 1988
Afghanistan: Part of Paktika and Kapisa provinces fall, as rebel pressure mounts against the Afghan Army. But the Mujahadin effort is too fragmented and the government holds on.

November 1988
4 India: An attempt by 400 Tamil mercenaries to overthrow the government of the Maldive Islands in the Indian Ocean is thwarted by Indian paratroops and commandos.

15 Tunisia: Palestine National Council of the PLO declare a Palestinian state in absentia.

December 1988
2 Pakistan: Benazir Bhutto becomes prime minister.

7 USSR: Gorbachev announces unilateral troop cuts of half a million men (10 per cent of Soviet military) over the next two years.

A soldier of 131 Independent Commando Squadron, Royal Engineers, weathers the sandstorm in the northern Kuwaiti desert.

1989
Ethiopia: A failed coup is followed by an army mutiny.

January 1989
Argentina: A left-wing group occupies a military barracks in Buenos Aires, but it is quickly dealt with after some fierce fighting in which more than 30 people are killed.
USSR: Gorbachev announces all chemical weapons will be destroyed, and defence spending will be cut by 14%.

11 Hungary: Political parties are authorised.
Sri Lanka: The state of emergency is finally lifted after five years.

19 Czechoslovakia: Riot police disperse

1980-1989

Sino-Vietnamese War 1980 · Iran-Iraq War 1980 · Iraq nuclear plant bombed 1981 · Falklands War 1982 · Israel invades Lebanon 1982 · US invades Grenada 1983

A soldier of 131 Independent Commando Squadron, Royal Engineers, weathers a sandstorm in the northern Kuwaiti desert.

demonstrators in Prague.

February 1989

Zaire: Student unrest is put down by security forces.

Poland: The government holds talks with the leaders of Solidarity.

3 Paraguay: The dictator Alfredo Stroessner is overthrown, after 34 years as president, by General Andres Rodriguez.

15 Afghanistan: The Soviet withdrawal is completed—with Lt-Gen Boris Gromov symbolically being the 'last man across' the Hairatan-Termez bridge. Soviet advisers remain to support Najibullah's regime.

19 Afghanistan: Najibullah proclaims martial law. Despite food shortages in Kabul, the expected collapse of his regime does not occur. The Mujahadin cannot produce an alternative government because of internal factions.

20 Ireland: On the UK mainland an IRA bomb devastates The Parachute Regiment's barracks in Shropshire.

26 Ireland: On 26 February Unionists reject offer of talks with the Irish premier.

28 Yugoslavia: Tanks move into Kosovo after a week of strikes by Albanians, who accuse the Serbs of trying to take control of the province.

March 1989

Zaire: Continued student unrest is put down by security forces.

10 Tibet: Bloody riots mark the anniversary of Chinese occupation.

IRA bomb Grand Hotel Brighton aiming for Mrs Thatcher **1984** | State of emergency declared in South Africa **1985** | Removal of Russian troops from Afghanistan starts **1986** | The Intifada begins in Gaza **1987** | SAS kill IRA cell in Gibraltar **1988** | Berlin Wall comes down **1989**

Z company of the Desert Rats on patrol, searching out alleged looters around a local oil refinery, south east of Basra, Iraq.

14 Lebanon: Many die in some of the worst fighting between Muslim and Christian militias for many months.

15 Hungary: Thousands demonstrate for freedom and democracy.

18 El Salvador: Elections are marred by fighting between troops and guerrillas. The right-wing Arena Party wins.

21 Ireland: Two senior RUC officers are killed by the IRA.

April 1989

Chad: A coup fails. One of its leaders is killed and the other, General Déby, flees to the Sudan from where he mounts guerrilla attacks.

2 Lebanon: Infter-Militia fighting continues with heavy local bombardments and sniping gun battles.

May 1989

Paraguay: General Andres Rodriguez who is freely elected.

2 Hungary: Hungarians begin dismantling their Austrian border fences.

4 China: A massive student demonstration takes place in Peking.

14 Israeli Peace Plan calls for a negotiating process with the Palestinians very similar to the one implemented by the Oslo accords.

17 Peru: 'Shining Path' terrorists kill 70 people in a single day.

18 China: Martial law is proclaimed. Students occupy the centre of the Peking, setting up bar-

1980-1989

Sino-Vietnamese War 1980 | Iran-Iraq War 1980 | Iraq nuclear plant bombed 1981 | Falklands War 1982 | Israel invades Lebanon 1982 | US invades Grenada 1983

The Berlin wall, former dividing line between East and West Germany, shortly before it was pulled down.

ricades. By mid-May there are some one million protesters including a large group of students on hunger strike in Tianamen Square.

June 1989
USSR: During the summer ethnic violence flares up in many of the Soviet republics.
3 Iran: Ayatollah Khomeini dies.
China: Troops attack the students and protesters in Tianamen Square, massacring some 2-5,000 throughout the city. Many more are also later arrested and executed.

18 Poland: Solidarity wins a sweeping victory in elections.

28 Sri Lanka: The Tamil Tigers agree to a cease-fire.

30 Sudan: There is a military coup.

July 1989
Afghanistan: The rebels are still repulsed at Jalalabad after many attempts to take the city since the Soviets left.
14 Somalia: Anti-government riots in Mogadishu lead to many deaths.

September 1989
18 Sri Lanka: Agreement is reached on withdrawal of Indian troops.

19 E Germany: A new democratic party is formed, eventually leading to resignation of Communist Erich Honecker. Political turmoil ensues.

22 Ireland: An IRA bomb kills ten Royal Marine bandsmen at Deal.

IRA bomb Grand Hotel Brighton aiming for Mrs Thatcher **1984** | State of emergency declared in South Africa **1985** | Removal of Russian troops from Afghanistan starts **1986** | The Intifada begins in Gaza **1987** | SAS kill IRA cell in Gibraltar **1988** | Berlin Wall comes down **1989**

29 Cambodia: The last Vietnamese troops leave after 10 years of occupation; advisers and technicians stay behind to help fight the Khmer Rouge.

A night to remember on November 11th 1989 as thousands of Berliners from east and west of the city celebrate the opening of the Berlin Wall 24 hours earlier.

November 1989
Lebanon: The Taif Accords are concluded to end the Lebanese civil war and legitimise the Syrian occupation.
10 Bulgaria: Todor Zhivkov is ousted in a coup as popular demonstrations herald an end to the Communist monopoly of power.
E Germany: The Berlin Wall is breached and all border crossings are opened.

16 El Salvador: Six Jesuit priests are murdered as the bitter civil war continues.

19 Czechoslovakia: A democratic opposition party is formed.

22 Lebanon: A massive car-bomb kills the president.

December 1989
3 USSR: At a superpower summit with US President Bush, Gorbachev declares the end of the Cold War.
20 Panama: US forces invade to topple dictator General Noriega and install Guillermo Endara as president in his place.

22 Romania: The dictator Nicolae Ceausescu is overthrown and captured. The revolutionaries set up a provisional government.

25 Romania: Ceausescu executed.

29 Czechoslovakia: Victor Havel is elected president as Communists quit.

1990-1999

- **1990** Invasion of Kuwait by Saddam Hussein
- **1991** First Gulf War
- **1992** Fighting erupts in Azerbaijan
- **1993** Blackhawk Down in Somalia
- **1994** Russians send troops to Chechnya
- **1995** Heavy fighting in Balkan Civil War

1990

Lebanon: With Syrian help, President Elias Hrawi defeats Iraqi-backed General Michel Aoun, who surrenders.

January 1990
Sudan: More than 600 are reported killed after religious clashes.
7 USSR: Troops are deployed in the Caucasus to prevent violence.

February 1990
2 Estonia: Independence from the Soviet Union is declared.
S Africa: Nelson Mandela is released and the ban on the ANC is lifted.

25 Nicaragua: The Sandinistas lose the elections.

26 Czechoslovakia: Soviet troops begin to withdraw.

More than a million citizens of the German Democratic Republic streamed across the openec border to West Berlin when the wall was brought down. Marking the reunion of the two countires.

March 1990
10 Haiti: A coup takes place.
11 Chile: General Pinochet hands over power to a civilian government.
Lithuania: Independence from the Soviet Union is declared.

18 E Germany: Free elections are held.

April 1990
Chad: Rebel incursions are led by General Idriss Déby from bases in the Sudan.
Kuwait: From now until July Saddam Hussein threatens Kuwait, demanding the surrender of the Bubiyan and Warbah Islands, and certain

US peacekeeping troops into Bosnia **1996**
Taliban captures Kabul **1996**
Tony Blair meets a Sinn Fein delegation **1997**
Good Friday Agreement **1998**
UN sanctions related to bin Laden come into force **1999**
Russia withdraws recognition of the Chechen government **1999**

Jubilant crowds outside the South African embassy in Trafalgar Square, London, celebrating the announcement that Nelson Mandela would be released.

disputed oilfields in northern Kuwait. He also wants concessions on the repayment of loans incurred during the Iran-Iraq War.

6 Nepal: From now to 19 April there are pro-democracy demonstrations.

May 1990
4 Latvia: Independence from the USSR declared.
20 Israel: The Arab Intifada continues and seven people are murdered in the Gaza Strip.

26 Cameroon: Anti-government riots.

27 Burma: The democrats win elections.

29 USSR: Boris Yeltsin is elected president.

30 Nicaragua: Contra rebels agree to disarm.

31 Yugoslavia: Non-Communist governments are elected in Slovenia and Croatia.

June 1990
2 Yugoslavia: Slovenia claims sovereignty.

July 1990
25 Liberia: 500 people are massacred in a church in the capital, Monrovia.

August 1990
2 Gulf War: On 2 August Iraqi forces invade and occupy Kuwait.

5 Gulf War: President Bush declares invasion "will not stand."

6 Gulf War: King Fahd meets Richard Cheney, requestsing US military assistance.

8 Gulf War: Iraq formally annexes Kuwait.

1990-1999

- Invasion of Kuwait by Saddam Hussein **1990**
- First Gulf War **1991**
- Fighting erupts in Azerbaijan **1992**
- Blackhawk Down in Somalia **1993**
- Russians send troops to Chechnya **1994**
- Heavy fighting in Balkan Civil War **1995**

U.S. Air force fighter planes arrive in Saudi Arabia.

9 USA: President Bush activates forces— probably some 425,000 in total—and begins moving them to Saudi Arabia, as do other allies such as Great Britain and France.
23 Armenia: The country declares its independence from USSR.

28 Iraq: Having invaded Kuwait Saddam Hussein matches the UN's blockade and sanctions by deploying more than 670,000 troops, threatening to use hostages as 'human shields', and looting Kuwait.

September 1990
10 Liberia: President Doe is killed.

October 1990
3 Germany: East and West Germany are reunited.

US amry soldiers from the 82nd Airborne carry a mock injured soldier on a stretcher to a helicopter during a training exercise in the Saudi desert.

8 Israel: Arab demonstrators are killed in Jerusalem.
21 Gulf War: Colin Powell flies to Riyadh to discuss forthcoming offensive plans.

31 Gulf War: Bush decides to double the US forces in Saudi Arabia

November 1990
10 Chad: Déby's troops invade.

29 Chad: Déby's troops capture Abeche—the French do not intervene.
Gulf War: UN Security Council authorises use of force to eject Iraq from Kuwait.

December 1990
Yugoslavia: A referendum shows that the

US peacekeeping troops into Bosnia **1996** | Taliban captures Kabul **1996** | Tony Blair meets a Sinn Fein delegation **1997** | Good Friday Agreement **1998** | UN sanctions related to bin Laden come into force **1999** | Russia withdraws recognition of the Chechen government **1999**

US army soldiers from 159th Aviation Regiment Fort Bragg, NC, decontaminate a Chinook CH-47D helicopter dressed in full chemical protective clothing.

population favours independence, while the new Croatian constitution points to secession.

1 Chad: President Habr flees to Cameroon. Déby takes Ndjamena. 2

3 Chad: Déby declares himself president.

4 Bangladesh: President Ershad is forced to resign.

6 Gulf War: First US ship carrying equipment arrives in Saudi Arabia.

9 Poland: Lech Walesa is elected president following local elections.

15 India: Many die in communal violence in Hyderabad and elsewhere.

1991

January 1991

Angola: From January to July the Cubans withdraw 50,000 troops as part of the peace settlement.

Ethiopia: At the beginning of the year loyalist troops continue to be forced back on all fronts and the fighting reaches Addis Ababa.

Somalia. Civil War. The year opens with an upsurge of opposition to government oppression by the guerrillas of the Somali National Movement (SNM), whose successes spark a popular insurrection in Mogadishu; fighting soon spreads throughout the country. Despite initial government success, the rebels soon gain the upper hand.

5 Gulf War: President Bush warns Iraq to withdraw from Kuwait or face the consequences.

1990-1999

- Invasion of Kuwait by Saddam Hussein **1990**
- First Gulf War **1991**
- Fighting erupts in Azerbaijan **1992**
- Blackhawk Down in Somalia **1993**
- Russians send troops to Chechnya **1994**
- Heavy fighting in Balkan Civil War **1995**

Oil fields continue to burn in Kuwait behind an abandoned Russian-built Iraqi tank after Operation Desert Storm during the Gulf War.

6 Gulf War: Saddam Hussein promises the 'mother of all battles'

11 Lithuania: The Soviet Army cracks down in Vilnius, the capital, with tanks and paratroops, many civilians are killed and wounded. After further clashes the population votes for independence.

12 Gulf War: The US Congress authorises the use of military force.

14 Iraq: The Iraq National Assembly votes for war.

15 Gulf War: The UN deadline for Iraqi forces to quit Kuwait expires at midnight (0500 GMT). Bush decides to use the military option and Operation 'Desert Storm' begins.

16 Iraq: The Allied air offensive begins. The Iraqis fire SCUD missiles at both Saudi Arabia and Israel. Coalition forces capture Qarah Island, 20 miles off coast, and nearby tiny Umm al-Maradim Island.

17 Gulf War: Allied attack begins with Apache strike.

18 Iraq: 12 Iraqi SCUD missiles land in Israel. First American air attacks are launched from Turkey.

19 Gulf War: Some Coalition pilots shot down.

20 Latvia: Soviet 'black beret' interior ministry troops storm a police academy in Riga.

23 Gulf War: British high command, alarmed at aircraft losses, abandons low-altitude attacks

| 1996 US peacekeeping troops into Bosnia | 1996 Taliban captures Kabul | 1997 Tony Blair meets a Sinn Fein delegation | 1998 Good Friday Agreement | 1999 UN sanctions related to bin Laden come into force | 1999 Russia withdraws recognition of the Chechen government |

A US soldier keeps guard as Kuwaiti citizens celebrate on the roof top of the local police station near Kuwait City, during the Gulf War.

against airfields.

24 Gulf War: Intense attacks against Iraqi aircraft shelters begin.

27 Somalia: Rebels capture the capital.

29 Iraq: On 29 January the Coalition achieve air supremacy.
Iraqi forces launch two small attacks through the Obstacle Belt near al Wafra, and then capture the small Saudi oil town of Khafji. It is recaptured the following day.

February 1991

Somalia: Rebels form a provisional government.

1 Gulf War: Tomahawk missiles launched in attack on Baghdad airfield.

2 Gulf War: Schwarzkopf decides against amphibious landing in Kuwait.

3 Gulf War: First battleship gunfire against targets in Kuwait.

6 Thailand: General Sunthorn Kongsompong imposes direct military rule.
Gulf War: US VII corps arrival in theatre complete.

7 Ireland: The IRA fires a mortar bomb 15 yards from a room where Prime Minister John Major is meeting with his cabinet. No one is injured.

8 Gulf War: Cheney and Powell fly to Riyadh for final review of ground war plans.

11 Israel: Complaints about the effectiveness of the US Patriot missiles, given to defend

1990-1999

- **1990** Invasion of Kuwait by Saddam Hussein
- **1991** First Gulf War
- **1992** Fighting erupts in Azerbaijan
- **1993** Blackhawk Down in Somalia
- **1994** Russians send troops to Chechnya
- **1995** Heavy fighting in Balkan Civil War

A group of Iraqi soldiers hold their hands up as they arrive at a US military check point at Nasiriyah, 300km from Baghdad, after the end of the Gulf War.

against Scud attacks.

16 Gulf War: VII Corps moves into final attack positions.

18 Ireland: The IRA terror bombing campaign continues with a bomb explosion outside Victoria Station, London.

Gulf War: USS *Tripoli* and USS *Princeton* strike mines.

20 Gulf War: 1st Cavalry Division feints up the Wadi al Batin; pulls back with three dead and nine wounded.

22 Gulf War: Marines begin infiltrating into Kuwait.

23 Gulf War: Army Special Forces teams inserted deep into Iraq. Stealth fighters attack targets.

24 Gulf War: Operation 'Desert Sabre' begins. Coalition forces advance against minimal Iraqi opposition and make rapid gains.

25 Gulf War: A Scud missile destroys a barracks in Al Khobar, killing 28 Americans and wounding 98.

26 Gulf War: Iraqis flee Kuwait City. VII Corps rocks Republican Guard in Battle of 73 Easting.

27 Gulf War: Coalition forces enter Kuwait City.

28 Gulf War: Iraqi forces fleeing Kuwait are caught along the Basra road; thousands of Iraqi tanks, vehicles and guns destroyed. By the end of the day hostilities have ended.

US peacekeeping troops into Bosnia **1996** Taliban captures Kabul **1996** Tony Blair meets a Sinn Fein delegation **1997** Good Friday Agreement **1998** UN sanctions related to bin Laden come into force **1999** Russia withdraws recognition of the Chechen government **1999**

March 1991

Iraq: Internal problems in Iraq include Shi'ite revolt in the south begins but is savagely suppressed by the Republican Guards.

2 Gulf War: 24th Inf Div attacks Hammurabi Division as it flees; destroys over 600 vehicles.

3 Iraq: There is a formal cease-fire as Schwarzkopf meets Iraqi generals at Safwan and, eight days later UNIKOM (United Nations Kuwait Observation Mission) is authorised.

21 Ethiopia: The government collapses and Mengistu flees the country.

26 Mali: President Traore is ousted after 150 die in riots.

29 Ethiopia: The rebels occupy the capital and set up a new government.

A long line of vehicles, including an Iraqi Russian-built tank, stand abandoned by fleeing Iraqi troops on the outskirts of Kuwait City.

April 1991

Iraq: There is a Kurdish uprising in the north, where Iraqi troops capture Kurdish-held towns, forcing hundreds of thousands to seek refuge in the mountains. British, French and American troops are sent in to help prepare camps in 'safe havens'.

9 USSR: The Republic of Georgia declares its independence, and later in the month there is increasing border violence between Armenia and Azerbaijan.

11 Ireland: A police undercover team kill a terrorist during a mortar attack in Downpatrick.

15 Peru: There is an extension of emergency

1990-1999

- Invasion of Kuwait by Saddam Hussein **1990**
- First Gulf War **1991**
- Fighting erupts in Azerbaijan **1992**
- Blackhawk Down in Somalia **1993**
- Russians send troops to Chechnya **1994**
- Heavy fighting in Balkan Civil War **1995**

Part of the squadron of Jaguar ground attack attack aircraft based at RAF Coltishall.

measures after further terrorist violence.

May 1991

Balkans: The widespread violence in Croatia is getting steadily worse, especially in eastern Croatia and Dalmatia.

6 S Africa: Some 60 people die in the bloodiest clashes of township violence for some time.

31 Angola: Warring factions sign a peace treaty.
Ireland: Three UDR soldiers die and thirteen are injured when a car-bomb hits their barracks.

4 UK: Under 'Options for Change' the government announces a fundamental restructuring of the army, reducing it to 116,000.

25 Yugoslavia: Slovenia and Croatia declare independence.

27 Yugoslavia: Federal forces (JNA—Jugoslav National Army) move to secure Slovenia's borders. Within a month both Federal and irregular forces are engaged in allout war in neighbouring Croatia.

June 1991

1 Haiti: Some 200 are killed in a military coup led by General Raoul Cedras, which forces the democratically elected President Aristide to flee the country.

July 1991

UK: It is decided to reduce the Brigade of Gurkhas from 8,000 to 2,500 by 1997.

1 Lebanon: Lebanese troops surround the

US peacekeeping troops into Bosnia **1996**

Taliban captures Kabul **1996**

Tony Blair meets a Sinn Fein delegation **1997**

Good Friday Agreement **1998**

UN sanctions related to bin Laden come into force **1999**

Russia withdraws recognition of the Chechen government **1999**

A Jaguar Jet takes off for the Gulf from RAF Coltishall in Norfolk.

PLO camp at Ein Helwe, then launch a full-scale offensive to flush the PLO out of the foothills east of Sidon.

August 1991
Latvia: Latvia declares its independence.

4 W Sahara: There is renewed fighting between Moroccan troops and the Polisaro Front rebels.

10 Latvia: Independence recognised by the USSR.

19 USSR: an attempted coup in Moscow against Gorbachev fails, thanks mainly to Boris Yeltsin, president of the Russian republic.

September 1991
10 Estonia/Latvia: The USSR recognises full independence of both countries

25 Yugoslavia: UN Security Council implements an arms embargo and starts to create UNPROFOR.

October 1991
12 Yugoslavia: Dubrovnik is shelled.

27 USSR: Despite hostile resolutions of the Russian Duma and threats from President Yeltsin, parliamentary and presidential elections are held in Chechnya, and Dudayev is elected president.

November 1991
2 Ireland: Two are killed and others wounded in bomb attack on a military hospital.

7 USSR: Yeltsin declares a state of emergency in Chechnya and orders Dudayev's arrest.

1990-1999

- Invasion of Kuwait by Saddam Hussein **1990**
- First Gulf War **1991**
- Fighting erupts in Azerbaijan **1992**
- Blackhawk Down in Somalia **1993**
- Russians send troops to Chechnya **1994**
- Heavy fighting in Balkan Civil War **1995**

Smoke and flames pour out from the harbour and inside the walled city of Dubrovnik, after the Croatian town suffered heavy bombardment by the Yugoslavian Federal army.

9 Chechnya: Russian troops fly into Khankala Airport outside Grozny, where they are immediately blockaded by a new Chechen national guard. A huge mass meeting in Grozny rallies around the Dudayev government. Meanwhile, with the rivalry between Yeltsin and Gorbachev still proceeding, Gorbachev orders that Russian and Soviet troops should stay neutral.

16 Ireland: Two bombers die in a premature bomb explosion at St Albans.

19 Yugoslavia: The Croatian city of Vukovar falls to the Serbs and fighting escalates.

December 1991

9 Kuwait: A US-Kuwait Defence Agreement is signed.

31 USSR (CIS): By the end of the year the Soviet Union has ceased to exist and in its place there is a fragile federation' The Commonwealth of Independent States' (CIS), and Gorbachev has resigned.

1992

January 1992

This year marks the beginning of the secessionist revolt of Abkhazia against Georgia.

1 El Salvador: A peace is signed to end the bitter twelve-year civil war which has led to the deaths of 75,000 people.

2 Balkans: The 15th Serbo-Croat cease-fire is announced.

3 Chad: Government forces launch a counter-

US peacekeeping troops into Bosnia **1996**
Taliban captures Kabul **1996**
Tony Blair meets a Sinn Fein delegation **1997**
Good Friday Agreement **1998**
UN sanctions related to bin Laden come into force **1999**
Russia withdraws recognition of the Chechen government **1999**

Boris Yeltsin of the Russian Federation addresses officers of the Baltic fleet, during a visit to the military naval shipyard.

attack on rebels; France sends in paratroops.

5 Somalia: UN mediation fails to end civil war which has claimed at least 20,000 lives since November 1991. One side is led by acting president Ali Mahdi Mohammed, the other by General Farah Aidid.

9 Balkans: The Serbs declare their own republic.

14 Balkans: UN observers arrive in Croatia and recommend a peace-keeping force of some 14,000.

15 Balkans: The European Community recognises Croatia and Slovenia.

17 Ireland: Teebane Crossroads—Seven Protestant constructions workers at a security base in Co Tyrone are killed by an IRA bomb.
26 Azerbaijan: Heavy fighting with Armenia erupts over Nagorno-Karabakh.

February 1992
4 Venezuela: Rebel army tank units are crushed.

6 Guatemala: The government and rebels open talks to end the civil war.

15 Israel: A Palestine commando group breaks into an army barracks and kills three soldiers.

17 Ireland: The worst single IRA attack since 1988 takes place; seven Protestants are killed and seven wounded.

19 Germany: The government lifts the ban against German troops serving abroad which

1990-1999

- **1990** Invasion of Kuwait by Saddam Hussein
- **1991** First Gulf War
- **1992** Fighting erupts in Azerbaijan
- **1993** Blackhawk Down in Somalia
- **1994** Russians send troops to Chechnya
- **1995** Heavy fighting in Balkan Civil War

British soldiers erect a perimeter fence at their base in Tomislavgrad to be used as an intermediate base for the supply convoys on their way to Vitez.

has been in force since 1949.

March 1992

1 Balkans: The first barricades go up in Sarajevo.
16 Balkans: UNPROFOR advance parties arrive and begin setting up bases.

26 Balkans: Fighting erupts in Bosanski Brod.

27 Balkans: The Bosnian Serbs proclaim their own constitution.

31 Chechnya: Chechen opposition forces, backed and armed by Russia, attempt an armed coup in Grozny, but are driven out.

April 1992

UK: The Adjutant General's Corps is established.
Balkans: There is fighting in northern Bosnia.

15 Afghanistan: General Najibullah's government collapses, with increased fighting by the Mujahadin, whose leader, Sibghatullah Mojaddedi, takes over as interim president after a UN-brokered peace deal.

21 Balkans: There is widespread fighting in Sarajevo.

27 Balkans: Serbia and Montenegro proclaim a new Yugoslav state.

30 Balkans: Bridges connecting Bosnia and Croatia at Brcko and Bosanski Samac are destroyed.

Balkans: The EC withdraws its ambassadors from Belgrade in protest at the continued siege of Sarajevo, and later that month EC, Red Cross and UN peacekeepers all have to pull

US peacekeeping troops into Bosnia **1996** · Taliban captures Kabul **1996** · Tony Blair meets a Sinn Féin delegation **1997** · Good Friday Agreement **1998** · UN sanctions related to bin Laden come into force **1999** · Russia withdraws recognition of the Chechen government **1999**

Sapper Michael Griffins from Levenshulme, on guard duty at the Tomslavgrad Depot of the British Army UN relief effort in Croatia.

out of the besieged city. Harrowing pictures from Sarajevo bring pressure for world-wide sanctions against the Serbs. The UN vote for these sanctions to be implemented.

September 1992
6 Dagestan: Russian special forces and other armed units enter a Dagestan border village preparing to enter Chechnya, but they are forced to retreat by the local population.

November 1992
There is a bloody clash between the Ingush Republic and Ossetia over the Prigorodny district, which had originally belonged to the Chechen-Ingush autonomous republic but had been handed over by the Stalin government of the Soviet Union to North Ossetia after the mass deportations of 1944. Russia basically sides with Ossetia,

December 1992
Burhanuddin Rabbani is declared president under a multi-party accord.
Chechenya: The Yeltsin administration decides to step up its support of forces in Chechnya opposed to the Dudayev government.

1993

January 1993
Zaire: In Kinshasa troops riot over pay, and kill foreigners including the French Ambassador.
Angola: There is renewed fighting.
Balkans: Early in the month UN proposals to partition Bosnia are rejected. Horrific reports of 'ethnic cleansing' by BosnianSerb forces shock the world. An EC report includes evidence of 20,000 rapes of Bosnian women.

1990-1999

- **1990** Invasion of Kuwait by Saddam Hussein
- **1991** First Gulf War
- **1992** Fighting erupts in Azerbaijan
- **1993** Blackhawk Down in Somalia
- **1994** Russians send troops to Chechnya
- **1995** Heavy fighting in Balkan Civil War

King Hussein of Jordan meets Prime Minister Margaret Thatcher at 10 Downing Street, in London.

3 Russia: Presidents Bush and Yeltsin sign the START-2 Treaty, ending the Cold War.

7 Israel: Israel eases its stance towards the Hamas deportees whom they had isolated in no man's land in southern Lebanon.
Somalia: The first major operation by US forces against the Somali warlord General Aidid begins.
Balkans: Canadian peace-keepers arrive in Macedonia to patrol the border with Serbia and Albania to prevent the spread of the war.

8 Tajikistan: A state of emergency is declared; Russian troops are under attack from fundamentalists operating from Afghanistan.

15 France: At the UNESCO headquarters, 130 countries sign a chemical disarmament treaty which forbids the possession and manufacture of these weapons of mass destruction. The destruction of stockpiles held by such countries as USA and Russia will be supervised by UN representatives.
20 Angola: Jonas Savimbi's UNITA rebels take the important oil town of Sayo.

27/28 Ireland: A bomb at Harrods in London, which injures four people, marks the fourth time the IRA have bombed the famous store. More bombs on the mainland include Camden.

February 1993

1 Cambodia: Government forces launch an offensive against the Khmer Rouge in west and north central Cambodia.

17 Lebanon: There is heavy fighting between Israeli forces and pro-Iranian guerrillas.

US peacekeeping troops into Bosnia **1996** | Taliban captures Kabul **1996** | Tony Blair meets a Sinn Fein delegation **1997** | Good Friday Agreement **1998** | UN sanctions related to bin Laden come into force **1999** | Russia withdraws recognition of the Chechen government **1999**

A member of the Queen's Royal Lancers in the Gulf, examining his weapons.

20 Cambodia: On the 20th the UN decide to send 16,000 troops to enforce the cease-fire.

March 1993
3 Mozambique: UN peacekeepers arrive to keep peace between government and RENAMO.
7 Afghanistan: The warlords sign a peace accord.

30 UK: IRA bomb goes off in Warrington.

April 1993
Azerbaijan: By early April Armenian forces have taken a tenth of the country, including the town of Kelbadzhar, and are now attacking Fizuli with tanks and artillery. Armenia says that the fighting is the work of 'Karabakh self-defence forces' rather than of their troops.

24 UK: Bishopsgate bomb—An IRA bomb containing one ton of fertilizer explosives goes off at the NatWest Tower in London. One is killed and 30 are injured. Damages amount to $1 billion.
26 Somalia: US troops begin to depart, after handing over to UN Pakistani peace-keepers.

May 1993
4 Cambodia: The Khmer Rouge ambush a UN convoy and attack a UN camp.

15 Balkans: UN peace proposals are rejected by Bosnian-Serbs, who claim to control of 70% of Bosnia which they have 'ethnically cleansed'.

June 1993
Azerbaijan: President Abulfaz Elchibey is overthrown by a coup with Russian help.
Liberia: More than 270 people are killed by rebel forces near Monrovia.

1990-1999

- Invasion of Kuwait by Saddam Hussein **1990**
- First Gulf War **1991**
- Fighting erupts in Azerbaijan **1992**
- Blackhawk Down in Somalia **1993**
- Russians send troops to Chechnya **1994**
- Heavy fighting in Balkan Civil War **1995**

A Serbian soldier searches for a pistol from a Croatian prisoner amongst the ruined buildings of Vukovar.

4 Balkans: Russia agrees to send 5,000 troops to help the UN protect six 'safe havens'.

5 Somalia: UN peace-keepers are killed by troops loyal to Aidid.
17 Somalia: Raid by US ground troops and helicopter gunships fails to capture Aidid.

25 Spain: ETA bombers kill five senior military officers in Madrid.

30 Azerbaijan: The rebel leader, Colonel Huseynov, is appointed prime minister.

July 1993
13 Afghanistan: Tajik rebels, out of Afghanistan, kill 25 in Russian army posts.

September 1993
9 Somalia: Many are killed by gunships when rescuing UN troops from hostile crowds.

13 Israel: Israel and the PLO sign an agreement for limited Palestinian autonomy.
16 Angola: The UN decides to impose sanctions against UNITA.

28 Russia: The rebel-held White House in Moscow is surrounded by government forces.

October 1993
Burundi: Civil war erupts between Hutu and Tutsi tribes, with many civilian deaths.
3

4 Russia: Many are killed on 4 October when Yeltsin orders troops to storm the Moscow White House.

5 Somalia: A US raid goes wrong and a number of soldiers are killed and wounded.

US peacekeeping troops into Bosnia **1996** | Taliban captures Kabul **1996** | Tony Blair meets a Sinn Fein delegation **1997** | Good Friday Agreement **1998** | UN sanctions related to bin Laden come into force **1999** | Russia withdraws recognition of the Chechen government **1999**

23 Ireland: Shankhill bomb—IRA detonates a bomb in a Belfast fish shop. Ten people die including one of the bombers; 57 are injured.

December 1993
15 UK: John Major and Albert Reynolds sign a historic peace agreement, which they hope will be the first step towards ending the violence. They issue a Joint Declaration on Northern Ireland which says "the ending of divisions can come about only through the agreement and co-operation of the people, North and South, representing both traditions in Ireland."

1994

January 1994
Afghanistan: Factional fighting resurfaces leaving the mujahedin badly divided.
Belgium. In January NATO leaders endorse President Clinton's 'Partnership for Peace' plan for closer military co-operation with East

Rwandan refugees, carrying wood, pass by a body (foreground) as they return to the Kikumba refugee camp, 30km north of Goma, Zaire.

European countries.
2 Mexico: The Zapatista 'Army of National Liberation' rebels seize five towns in Ciapas.

5 Balkans: Lieutenant-General Sir Michael Rose, a British SAS commander, is appointed to command UN forces in Bosnia.

10 Balkans: Bosnian and Croatian leaders agree to a cease-fire.

11 Ireland: IRA carbomb in Crossmaglen injures two British soldiers. The Irish government lifts its broadcasting ban on Sinn Fein.

16 S Africa: The PanAfrican Congress says that it is ending its armed struggle.

27 Lithuania: Lithuania is the ex-communist

1990-1999

- **1990** Invasion of Kuwait by Saddam Hussein
- **1991** First Gulf War
- **1992** Fighting erupts in Azerbaijan
- **1993** Blackhawk Down in Somalia
- **1994** Russians send troops to Chechnya
- **1995** Heavy fighting in Balkan Civil War

Lt Gen Sir Michael Rose, Commander of the UN Forces in Bosnia, speaks to the press after the announcement of the withdrawal of Serbian forces around Sarajevo.

country first to join the 'Partnership for Peace'.

February 1994

Ghana: In February more than 1,000 people are killed and 70 villages razed in ethnic fighting.

1 Burundi: 50 people killed in clashes between Hutus and Tutsis

5 Balkans: 68 civilians are killed and 200 wounded in mortar attack on Sarajevo market.

7 Afghanistan: After six days of vicious fighting, factions in Kabul agree to a cease-fire.

17 Greece: The border with Macedonia is closed.

18 Balkans: Serb forces pull back from around Sarajevo under the threat of NATO air strikes.

Ireland: Loyalist gunmen kill three in Belfast and on the following day the IRA firebomb seven Central London stores.

25 Israel: On the West Bank in Hebron gunmen shoot 30 worshippers in a mosque.

28 Balkans: NATO troops shoot down four Serb fighter aircraft.

March 1994

5 Israel: There are peace demonstrations by 50,000 young Jews and Arabs.

7 Burundi: Many Hutus are massacred by the Tutsi-dominated army.

11 S Africa: Riots, looting and gun battles take

1996	1996	1997	1998	1999	1999
US peacekeeping troops into Bosnia	Taliban captures Kabul	Tony Blair meets a Sinn Fein delegation	Good Friday Agreement	UN sanctions related to bin Laden come into force	Russia withdraws recognition of the Chechen government

Outside Kigali City local people receive aid from the International Red Cross.

place in Bophuthatswana 'homeland'.

13 Ireland: London Heathrow is shut by IRA mortar attack.

17 Cambodia: Government forces seize the Khymer Rouge HQ at Pailin.

25 Somalia: The remaining US troops leave, handing over to UN troops from Egypt and Pakistan; the two main warlords sign a peace pact.

28 S Africa: Gun battles rage in Johannesburg between Zulus and ANC supporters.

29 Guatemala: The government and rebel groups sign a peace agreement.

April 1994

Hamas carries out suicide bombings in Israeli towns of Afula and Hadera: 13 dead, 80 wounded.

7 Rwanda: There are riots in Kigali following the deaths of the presidents of Burundi and Rwanda in an air crash. Anarchy sweeps the country and thousands are killed. Belgian paratroops are sent in to rescue expatriate families.

22 Balkans: The UN approve the sending of more troops as peace talks founder.

May 1994

Palestine: Yasser Arafat arrives in Gaza.
Chechnya: There is an attempt to assassinate Dudayev with a remote-controlled car bomb.

10 S Africa: Nelson Mandela becomes president.

16 Armenia/Azerbaijan: A cease-fire is agreed in disputed Nagorno-Karabakh.

21 Aden: North Yemeni forces advance on

1990-1999

- **1990** Invasion of Kuwait by Saddam Hussein
- **1991** First Gulf War
- **1992** Fighting erupts in Azerbaijan
- **1993** Blackhawk Down in Somalia
- **1994** Russians send troops to Chechnya
- **1995** Heavy fighting in Balkan Civil War

Hercules aircraft are prepared for service in Bosnia at RAF Lyneham, Wiltshire.

Aden as secession is proclaimed.

25 S Africa: The UN lifts arms embargo on South Africa.

31 Rwanda: By the end of the monthy the death toll has reached half a million and one and a half million are homeless.

June 1994

6 France. Large D-Day commemorations are held on 50th anniversary of landings.

July 1994

Rwanda: A small UN force attempts to evacuate people from Kigali.

4 Rwanda: Kigali is captured by rebel Rwandan Patriotic Front (RPF) forces.

7 Aden: Yemeni forces seize the port, but secessionist leaders vow to fight on.

14 UK: Drastic new reductions in the armed forces are announced.

24 Israel: Hamas suicide bomber blows up a Dan bus in Tel Aviv.

25 Israel: Jordan and Israel end the state of war that has existed for 46 years.

27 Balkans: The Serbs tighten their grip on Sarajevo and flout the ban on the use of heavy weapons at Gorazde.

August 1994

Rwanda: Hutus try to leave the country, fearing retaliation by the RPF. The Zairan town of Bukavu is swamped by 100,000 refugees.

31 Germany: The last Russian troops are

US peacekeeping troops into Bosnia **1996** | Taliban captures Kabul **1996** | Tony Blair meets a Sinn Fein delegation **1997** | Good Friday Agreement **1998** | UN sanctions related to bin Laden come into force **1999** | Russia withdraws recognition of the Chechen government **1999**

American and Russian forces serving together in Bosnia. This was the first time the two Countries forces have done so since World war Two.

leaving (and from Estonia and Latvia).
Ireland: An IRA cease-fire brings hopes of peace after 25 years of killings.

September 1994
8 Germany: The last Allied soldiers leave Berlin.

19 Haiti: US troops seize the island without a shot being fired.

23 Turkey: A major military assault begins on the Kurdish guerrilla stronghold in Tunceli province.

October 1994
Chechnya: Armed forces under the command of some elements of the Russian-backed opposition stage a surprise attack on Grozny and, without much fighting, occupy some administrative buildings.
Sri Lanka: Continuing trouble with Tamil Tigers halts peace.

10 Iraq: A build-up of Iraqi forces on the Kuwait border prompts immediate build-up of US forces there, and Saddam Hussein backs down.

13 Ireland: The Loyalists announce a cease-fire.

19 Israel: Hamas suicide bombing on a Tel Aviv bus kills 22, wounds 40.

26 Israel: Peace treaty signed between Jordan and Israel.

30 Balkans: The Bosnians launch a successful offensive in NW Bosnia, forcing the Serbs to flee, but they then counterattack around Bihac.

1990-1999

- Invasion of Kuwait by Saddam Hussein **1990**
- First Gulf War **1991**
- Fighting erupts in Azerbaijan **1992**
- Blackhawk Down in Somalia **1993**
- Russians send troops to Chechnya **1994**
- Heavy fighting in Balkan Civil War **1995**

Angolan government forces hold their weapons in ready while controlling the area, at the Huambo area.

November 1994

Balkans: NATO aircraft strike at Serb targets.
Afghanistan: The Taliban, backed by Pakistan begins to dominate.
10 Angola: The government forces overrun UNITA headquarters at Huambo.

20 Angola: A peace pact is signed to finally end the nineteen-year civil war.

24 Russia: An armoured force attempts to install a 'Government of National Rebirth' in Grozny. Russian television announces the Dudayev government has fled the Presidential Palace, but the attack is a fiasco. It is beaten back and 21 Russian soldiers are taken prisoner, exposing the real force behind the attack.
Chechnya: Start of the first Chechen war which lasts November 1994–November 1996

31 Ireland: The IRA announces that there will be a cessation of military operations in an effort to help the democratic peace process.

December 1994

11 Chechnya: The Russians send 30,000 troops with hundreds of tanks into the breakaway rebel republic, but they are faced by Chechen guerrillas, who defend Grozny during bitter fighting for the rest of the month.

31 Chechnya: The Russian forces bombard Grozny, and push into the city with a strong armored force. The city suffers massive destruction, but the invading forces suffer a bloody defeat.

1995

January 1995

Chechnya: In January the Russian Army continues to pound Grozny in a new offensive.

| 1996 US peacekeeping troops into Bosnia | 1996 Taliban captures Kabul | 1997 Tony Blair meets a Sinn Fein delegation | 1998 Good Friday Agreement | 1999 UN sanctions related to bin Laden come into force | 1999 Russia withdraws recognition of the Chechen government |

Minister of Defence, Svend Aage Jensby, announced that two Danish F-16 dropped bombs against targets in Afghanistan.

Chechen rebels take 2,000 Russians hostage in a hospital in Budyonnovsk, but release them after having used some as human shields to get back to safe territory.

1 Balkans: Another official cease-fire begins, but heavy fighting breaks out again the following month around the so-called safe havens of Bihac, Srebenica and Gorazde as the Serbs begin a 'spring offensive'.

3 Sri Lanka: The Tamil Tigers agree to a cease-fire.

February 1995

Burma: In February the last Karen rebel stronghold falls.

14 Pakistan: There is sectarian fighting in Karachi, and in March between Shi'ite and Sunni Muslims.

15 Ecuador: In mid-February a cease-fire ends border fighting with Peru, both sides claiming victory.

16 Thailand: The armed forces are put on full alert following border incursions by Burmese.

20 Somalia: US forces land to oversee withdrawal of remaining 2,500 UN troops from the civil war-torn country. Eighty AFVs are brought ashore plus 14,000 new UN troops to form a rearguard while the failed UN peace-keeping force is withdrawn. Somalia is being given up as a lost cause.

March 1995

Turkey: 35,000 Turkish troops enter N Iraq searching for Kurdish separatists.

1990-1999

- Invasion of Kuwait by Saddam Hussein **1990**
- First Gulf War **1991**
- Fighting erupts in Azerbaijan **1992**
- Blackhawk Down in Somalia **1993**
- Russians send troops to Chechnya **1994**
- Heavy fighting in Balkan Civil War **1995**

Hundreds of Islamics from the Pakistan main fundamentalists party, Jammat-i-Islami (JI) raise slogans against Russia for its offensive on Chechnya.

Ireland: In March-April there is an impasse in peace talks because of the IRA's refusal to surrender weapons as a pre-condition to all party talks.

6 Afghanistan: the government forces launch attacks on last rebel stronghold in the capital Kabul and two weeks later re-enter the town. The civil war has so far lasted for three years.

Balkans: Bosnia and Croatia sign pact to form common military front against the Serbs.

20 Japan: There is a nerve gas attacks against civilians in Tokyo and Yokohama underground railways.

27 Balkans: The UN again threatens air strikes if Serbs do not stop shelling UN 'safe areas'.

April 1995

Rwanda. In April more deaths and misery as the Rwandan Patriotic Front Army (Tutsis) try to close Kibeho refugee camp. Camps contain some 250,000 refugee Hutu, but also militiamen responsible for original massacre of Tutsi.

2 Israel: Nine people are killed in the Gaza Strip as Hamas members are preparing a bomb.

4 Balkans: There is heavy fighting around Tuzla as Bosmans begin their offensive.

9 Israel: Seven Israeli soldiers are killed by another suicide bomb.

19 Chechnya: Russian troops claim to have captured last Chechen stronghold.
USA: A massive car-bomb kills and injures hundreds in Oklahoma City.

US peacekeeping troops into Bosnia **1996** — Taliban captures Kabul **1996** — Tony Blair meets a Sinn Fein delegation **1997** — Good Friday Agreement **1998** — UN sanctions related to bin Laden come into force **1999** — Russia withdraws recognition of the Chechen government **1999**

French KFOR soldiers bring equipment for a Serb school in the village of Banja, about 70 km northwest from Pristina.

21 Japan: There are further nerve gas attacks against civilians in Tokyo and Yokohama underground railways.

May 1995
1 Sierra Leone: Rebel troops surround capital, Freetown.

2 Balkans: The Croatian capital Zagreb is shelled by the Serbs.

10 Israel: The Israelis release 250 Palestinian prisoners.

11 India: In Kashmir Indian troops break a two-month siege by Muslim separatist guerrillas, storming an Islamic shrine and killing 42.

26 Balkans: The Serbs take UN troops hostage to use as human shields against further air strikes, but later release them.

June 1995
28 Sri Lanka: Tamil rebels kill 161 people in five separate attacks.

July 1995
9 Sri Lanka: The government sends 10,000 troops against Tamil Tigers.

11 Balkans: The Serbs overrun Srebenica. UN troops are sent to protect Sarajevo.

August 1995
5 Balkans: The Croatian offensive inflicts major defeat upon the Serbs.

7 Sri Lanka: A Tamil suicide bomber kills 22 people in Colombo. Government forces recapture Jaffna, the Tamil Tigers' capital.

1990-1999

- Invasion of Kuwait by Saddam Hussein **1990**
- First Gulf War **1991**
- Fighting erupts in Azerbaijan **1992**
- Blackhawk Down in Somalia **1993**
- Russians send troops to Chechnya **1994**
- Heavy fighting in Balkan Civil War **1995**

Leah Rabin speaks to a crowd of tens of thousands of Israelis who gathered at Yitzhak Rabin Square in Tel Aviv 04 May, six months after he was assassinated by a Jewish extremist.

30 Balkans: NATO bombs Serb targets.

31 Ireland: The last day of August marks the first anniversary of the cease-fire. The IRA still refuse to hand in weapons.

September 1995

5 Mururoa Atoll: France conducts underground nuclear test, despite world-wide protests.

28 Israel: Israel agrees to give Palestinians autonomy on West Bank.

October 1995

1 Mururoa Atoll: France conducts a second underground nuclear test, despite world-wide protests.

13 Balkans: Bosnians and Croats besiege Serb stronghold of Banja Luka.

November 1995

4 Israel: Israeli PM Yitzhak Rabin assassinated by right-wing Israeli fanatic Yigal Amir.

21 Balkans: A Bosnian peace plan is agreed by the three national leaders. Under the agreement all armed groups in Bosnia will disband except for the authorised police. A 60,000-strong NATO force (IFOR) will be sent there after Christmas, to ensure that peace is kept.

December 1995

21 Israel: Israeli troops are withdrawn from Bethlehem.
Balkans: A peace accord is signed in Paris.

US peacekeeping troops into Bosnia **1996**
Taliban captures Kabul **1996**
Tony Blair meets a Sinn Fein delegation **1997**
Good Friday Agreement **1998**
UN sanctions related to bin Laden come into force **1999**
Russia withdraws recognition of the Chechen government **1999**

US Army soldiers walk in front of camouflage netted equipment as snow falls at their new base camp outside the Croatian border town of Zupanja.

1996

January 1996
2 Balkans: US Troops pour into Bosnia

5 Israel: Israeli security services assassinate Palestinian terrorist Yihyeh Ayash, 'The Engineer,' responsible for the death of over 60.

February 1996
UK: Canary Wharf bomb—The IRA announces the cease-fire will end. Scotland Yard receives warnings that a bomb is planted in the Canary Wharf area. At 7:01 PM a bomb explodes there killing two and injuring over a 100.

25 Israel: Hamas suicide bomber blows up a bus near Jerusalem's central bus station, killing 26 people and wounding 48 others. Less than an hour later, a second one explodes at a soldier's hitchhiking station near Ashkelon, killing one and injuring 31 others. The two attacks are said to be in retaliation for the slaying in Gaza of Yehiya Ayash.

March 1996
3 Israel: A Hamas suicide bomber blows up a bus on Jerusalem's Jaffa Road, killing 19 people and leaving at least 9 wounded.

4 Israel: A Hamas suicide bomb blows up Tel Aviv's Dizengoff Center, killing 13, including children, and wounding at least 130.

April 1996
21 Chechnya: Chechen President Dudayev is killed by a Russian rocket, which homes in on the signal from his satellite telephone.

1990-1999

- **1990** Invasion of Kuwait by Saddam Hussein
- **1991** First Gulf War
- **1992** Fighting erupts in Azerbaijan
- **1993** Blackhawk Down in Somalia
- **1994** Russians send troops to Chechnya
- **1995** Heavy fighting in Balkan Civil War

A building damaged by blast when a bomb went off in the vacinity of London's Canary Wharf.

May 1996
28 Chechnya: Yeltsin visits Chechnya and declares that Russia had destroyed all the "bandit groups" and won the war.

August 1996
6 Chechnya: The Chechens begin their successful attempt to retake Grozny from the Russian armed forces.
12 Dagestan: On behalf of the Yeltsin government, General Lebed begins serious negotiations with the Chechens at the border town of Khasavyurt in Dagestan.
31 Chechnya: All Russian troops have left Grozny, and an agreement

September 1996
Israel: The Al-Aksa tunnel riots—a false rumor spreads that a gate opened in an underground tunnel tourist attraction by the Israeli government, has endangered the foundations of the Al-Aqsa mosque. Several days of rioting and numerous casualties then ensue.
Afghanistan: Taliban captures Kabul, executes Najibullah and imposes its hardcore Islamic system.

November 1996
23 Russia: Russian Prime Minister Chernomyrdin and Maskhadov reach agreement on the withdrawal of Russian troops prior to Chechen presidential elections at the end of January 1997. In fact, the troops leave in six weeks. The first Chechen war is over.

1997

January 1997
18 Israel: Israelis and Palestinians reach agreement on Israeli redeployment in the West-Bank

- US peacekeeping troops into Bosnia **1996**
- Taliban captures Kabul **1996**
- Tony Blair meets a Sinn Fein delegation **1997**
- Good Friday Agreement **1998**
- UN sanctions related to bin Laden come into force **1999**
- Russia withdraws recognition of the Chechen government **1999**

city of Hebron.

March 1997
21 Israel: Cafe Apropos Bombing—a Hamas suicide bomber blows up the Cafe Apropos in central Tel Aviv, killing 3 Israelis and wounding 47 others.

July 1997
Afghanistan: Anti-Taliban forces led by Masood retake areas north of Kabul.

30 Israel: Two suicide bombers (Hamas and Islamic Jihad) strike in the Mahane Yehuda open-air market in Jerusalem, killing 12 and wounding at least 150 others.

September 1997
Jordan: Israeli agents bungle an attempt to kill Hamas terrorist leader Khald Mashaal in Jordan.

A file picture of London's Canary Wharf Tower which dominates the East London skyline. The highest building in Europe. The area around Canary Wharf was rocked this evening (Friday) with a bomb blast.

15 Ireland: Another IRA cease-fire is established and, for the first time since Ireland was divided in 1922, the Irish Free State, Ulster (British Province) and Sinn Fein, the political wing of the IRA, sit down to formal negotiations.

October 1997
13 Ireland: PM Tony Blair meets a Sinn Fein delegation and shakes hands with Martin McGuinness and Gerry Adams. The Protestant majority is outraged, citing the IRA's history of violence and refusal to lay down weapons.

December 1997
5 Ireland: A Catholic is killed outside Belfast, the first killing since the IRA cease-fire in July. The Loyalist Volunteer Force is suspected.

1990-1999

Invasion of Kuwait by Saddam Hussein **1990** · First Gulf War **1991** · Fighting erupts in Azerbaijan **1992** · Blackhawk Down in Somalia **1993** · Russians send troops to Chechnya **1994** · Heavy fighting in Balkan Civil War **1995**

1998

Sinn Fein president Gerry Adams outside No 10 with his delegates, after the peace talks with Prime Minister Tony Blair this afternoon.

January 1998

11 Ireland: On the eve of the talks resuming, Terry Enwright, a Roman Catholic doorman at a Belfast nightclub and nephew of Gerry Adams, is killed by the Loyalist Volunteer Force.

26 Ireland: The UDP leaves the peace talks rather than be expelled when the linked Ulster Freedom Fighters admit to recent murders.

29 Ireland: PM Tony Blair announces a judicial inquiry into the 1972 Bloody Sunday killings.

February 1998

20 Ireland: The Irish and British Governments temporarily expel Sinn Fein from the peace talks for two killings earlier in the month which are linked to the IRA.

April 1998

10 Ireland: After months of peace talks, murders and violence, the N Ireland peace talks produce the Good Friday Agreement.

May 1998

23 Ireland: A referendum on the historic Good Friday Agreement is voted on in N Ireland and the Republic. It passes by 71% to 29% in Northern Ireland; in the Republic 94% approve the compromise agreement.

August 1998

15 Ireland: 29 are killed and over 200 wounded by a bomb in Omagh—the most deadly paramilitary attack is blamed on the Real IRA.

September 1998

Afghanistan: US bombards extremist camps

- US peacekeeping troops into Bosnia **1996**
- Taliban captures Kabul **1996**
- Tony Blair meets a Sinn Fein delegation **1997**
- Good Friday Agreement **1998**
- UN sanctions related to bin Laden come into force **1999**
- Russia withdraws recognition of the Chechen government **1999**

British Prime Minister Tony Blair after the signing the historic agreement for peace in Northern Ireland.

to wipe out Saudi-born dissident Osama bin Laden, a guest of the Taliban. The Taliban gains control of 80% of the country, but is only recognised as the legal government by Pakistan, the United Arab Emirates and Saudi Arabia.

October 1998
Wye River Plantation talks result in an agreement for Israeli release of political prisoners and renewed Palestinian commitment.

16 Ireland: David Trimble and John Hume win the Nobel Peace Prize for their efforts to bring peace to Northern Ireland.

December 1998
18 Ireland: First steps in decommissioning terrorist weapons are taken when the Loyalist Volunteer Force hands over of a cache.

1999

April 1999
2 Ireland: On the first anniversary of the Good Friday Agreement, there is still no deal between the opposing sides.

May 1999
17 Israel: Labour party leader and former General Ehud Barak elected PM. Barak promises rapid progress towards peace.

July 1999
Chechnya: Chechen rebels associated with Shamil Basayev are the main force in raids by Islamic militants on Russian forces in Dagestan.

September 1999
Dagestan: The struggle heats up . Russian forces retaliate against the rebels and go on to stage attacks on Chechnya.

2000-2003

- A massive new Russian offensive in Grozny begins **2000**
- Israeli withdrawal from Lebanon **2000**
- Israeli PM Barak, US President Clinton and Palestinian Chairman Yasser Arafat meet at Camp David **2000**
- Palestinian riots after Israeli opposition leader Ariel Sharon visits the Temple Mount **2000**
- Ariel Sharon elected Prime Minister **2001**
- Taliban orders closure of UN offices in Kabul **2001**

Russian soldiers patrol streets in Chechen capital Grozny on Thursday, 09 March 2000.

October 1999
2 Chechnya: After a week of bombing Russian Vladimir Putin withdraws recognition of the Chechen government thus renouncing the Khasavyurt accords which ended the first Chechen war. Russia then invades Chechnya with large forces.

November 1999
UN sanctions related to bin Laden come into force. An embargo on air travel is imposed and Taliban assets abroad are frozen.

2000

January 2000
1 Russia: Boris Yeltsin resigns and Vladimir Putin becomes the acting president of Russia.

18 Chechnya: A massive new Russian offensive in Grozny begins against determined resistance. Heavy casualties on both sides.

May 2000
Lebanon: The Israeli withdrawal from Lebanon is finally completed.

July 2000
Israel: PM Barak, US President Clinton and Palestinian Chairman Yasser Arafat meet at Camp David in a failed attempt to hammer out a final settlement.

September 2000
Israel: Palestinians riot after Israeli opposition leader Ariel Sharon visits the Temple Mount, also the location of the Haram al Sharif and holy to Muslims. The violence escalates.

2001

9.11 Islamic Al-Qaeda group attacks on World Trade Center in NYC **2001**	Suicide bombings in Israel lead to operation Defensive Wall in the West Bank **2002**	Israel assassinates Saleh Shehadeh, head of Hamas. **2002**	American and British forces begin Gulf War 2 against Iraq. **2003**	Tikrit falls and the Coalition declares the war to be effectively over. **2003**	Palestinian Islam Jihad Suicide bomber kills 20 in Haifa. **2003**

(Left) A Russian soldier fixes a machinegun on the balcony of a destroyed building.
(Above) Russian soldiers returning from Chechnya.

February 2001
6 Israel: Right-wing Likud leader Ariel Sharon elected PM in Israel replacing Ehud Barak.

14 Afghanistan: UN announces thousands of people on verge of starvation in Afghanistan. The Taliban orders closure of UN offices in Kabul.

March 2001
1 Afghanistan: The Taliban provokes outrage by blowing up the Bamiyan Buddhas.

April 2001
Europe: Masood, leader of the Afghani opposition, visits Paris, Strasbourg and Brussels.

June 2001
Israel: Nightclub in Tel Aviv hit by suicide bomb, killing 20.

August 2001
9 Israel: Suicide bombing in Jerusalem by Islamic Jihad kills 15, wounds 130.

27 Israel: Israel assassinates Abu Ali Mustafa, Secretary General of the PFLP (Popular Front for the Liberation of Palestine).

September 2001
9 Afghanistan: A suicide-bomb attack against Masood is carried out using a video camera packed with explosives.

11 USA: Terror attacks on World Trade Center in NYC and the Pentagon carried out by Al-Qaeda headed by Osama Bin Laden, using civilian aircraft—with over 3,000 deaths. The US begins its war on terror.

2000-2003

- A massive new Russian offensive in Grozny begins **2000**
- Israeli withdrawal from Lebanon **2000**
- Israeli PM Barak, US President Clinton and Palestinian Chairman Yasser Arafat meet at Camp David **2000**
- Palestinian riots after Israeli opposition leader Ariel Sharon visits the Temple Mount **2000**
- Ariel Sharon elected Prime Minister **2001**
- Taliban orders closure of UN offices in Kabul **2001**

Israel: Israel and Palestinians agree to cease fire, but it is not implemented.

12 Europe: NATO invokes the mutual defense provision of its charter for the first time.

14 USA: Osama Bin Laden named as leading suspect in terror attacks on New York and Washington. Congress authorizes use of force against those responsible for 9/11 attacks.

15 Afghanistan: Masood is confirmed dead by opposition leaders. Taliban orders all foreigners to leave and warns of retaliation if any of its neighbours aid US attacks on Afghanistan.

19 USA: US forces begin deployment to Uzbekistan, Tajikistan, the Persian Gulf, and Diego Garcia. President Bush issues ultimatum to Taliban, demanding Osama bin Laden.

Afghanistan: Islamic clerics call on the Taliban

(Left) Vladimir Putin shakes hands with Bill Clinton. (Above) An Israeli forensic looks at bodies of victims on a passenger bus in Haifa, after a suicide bombing by the hardline Islamic group Hamas.

to ask bin Laden to leave the country voluntarily to avert war with the United States.

October 2001

1 India: Muslim militants kill 40 in an attack in Jammu and Kashmir.

7 Afghanistan: US begins air strikes on Taliban targets.

9 Afghanistan: US completes the destruction of Bin Laden's terrorist camps in Afghanistan.

15 USA: Postal anthrax attack.

17 Israel: In retaliation for death of Abu Ali Mustafa, the PFLP assassinates Israeli tourism minister Rehav'am Ze'evi. After the Palestine National Authority refuses to take action, Israeli

- **2001** 9-11 Islamic Al-Qaeda group attacks on World Trade Center in NYC
- **2002** Suicide bombings in Israel lead to operation Defensive Wall in the West Bank
- **2002** Israel assassinates Saleh Shehadeh, head of Hamas.
- **2003** American and British forces begin Gulf War 2 against Iraq.
- **2003** Tikrit falls and the Coalition declares the war to be effectively over.
- **2003** Palestinian Islam Jihad Suicide bomber kills 20 in Haifa.

Israeli policemen inspect the the body of one of two Palestinian suicide bombers in the northern Israeli town of Hadera.

enters Palestinian areas in the West Bank.

19 Afghanistan: Advance US ground operations begin.

28 Pakistan: Gunmen kill 16 at a Christian church service in Behawalpur, Pakistan

31 USA: Anthrax attack casualty dies.

November 2001
3 Afghanistan: The Taliban agree to UN-backed peace talks.
12 Afghanistan: Northern Alliance captures Kabul.

16 Afghanistan: Mohammed Atef, deputy of bin Laden, killed in a US air strike.

27 Afghanistan: Konduz prison rebellion suppressed with several hundred Taliban killed.

December 2001
1/2 Israel: Suicide bombings in Jerusalem kill 12 and Haifa 15.

3 Israel: Israel strikes back at the headquarters of the Palestinian Authority in Gaza.

11 Somalia: USA confirms that special forces are in Somalia providing 'counterterrorism support'.
12 Irael: Palestinian gunmen kill 10 in a bus ambush near Emmanuel.

13 India: Terrorist attack on Indian Parliament kills 12.

2002
Terrorist attacks continue in Israel with

2000-2003

- **A massive new Russian offensive in Grozny begins** 2000
- **Israeli withdrawal from Lebanon** 2000
- **Israeli PM Barak, US President Clinton and Palestinian Chairman Yasser Arafat meet at Camp David** 2000
- **Palestinian riots after Israeli opposition leader Ariel Sharon visits the Temple Mount** 2000
- **Ariel Sharon elected Prime Minister** 2001
- **Taliban orders closure of UN offices in Kabul** 2001

(Left) Saddam Hussein and Tarek Aziz.
(Above) An undated file photo shows Palestinian guerilla Sabri al-Banna, known as Abu Nidal, chief of the extremist Fatah-Revolutionary Council.

mounting casualties, eg: **17**/1 6 killed, 35 injured; **22**/1 2 killed, 40 injured at bus stop in Jerusalem; **5/2** 3 killed at Moshav Hamra; **16/2** 3 killed, 30 injured at pizzeria in Karnei Shomron; **18/2** 3 killed and 1 injured in attack on Gush Katif; **19/2** 6 soldiers killed and 1 injured in shooting attack near Ramallah; **2/3** 10 (incl 6 children) killed over 50 injured; **9/3** 11 killed, 54 injured by suicide bombing in Jerusalem café.

March 2002
Saudi Arabia: Prince Abdullah announces a peace plan—Israel withdraws from the occupied territories in return for Arab recognition.

Israel: Israel mounts Operation 'Defensive Wall' in the West Bank, arrests Palestinian leaders and enters the Jenin camp, where 50 people are killed. A proposed UN investigation is after Israel refuses to cooperate.

June 2002
24 USA: In a controversial speech President Bush calls for an Israeli withdrawal and a separate Palestinian state, but also insists that the PNA must first be reformed.

July 2002
23 Israel: Israel assassinates Saleh Shehadeh, head of Hamas.

August 2002
16 Iraq: Death of Sabri Banna (Abu Nidal), head of the Fatah Revolutionary Council by assassination or suicide in Baghdad.

October 2002
Libya: Libya withdraws from Arab League.

9-11 Islamic Al-Qaeda group attacks on World Trade Center in NYC **2001**

Suicide bombings in Israel lead to operation Defensive Wall in the West Bank **2002**

Israel assassinates Saleh Shehadeh, head of Hamas. **2002**

American and British forces begin Gulf War 2 against Iraq. **2003**

Tikrit falls and the Coalition declares the war to be effectively over. **2003**

Palestinian Islam Jihad Suicide bomber kills 20 in Haifa. **2003**

US Marines, members of 15 Marine Expeditionary Unit (MEU), in the port of Umm Qsar in southern Iraq.

2003

January 2003

Egypt: Conference of Palestinian group fails to agree on a cease-fire offer for Israel. Islamic movements claim the PLO no longer represents the Palestinian people.

28 Israel: Elections in Israel give wide margin of seats to the right-wing Likud party, returning PM Ariel Sharon for another term.

February 2003

Israel: Israel initiates a series of incursions in the Gaza strip and Nablus with numerous civilian casualties.

March 2003

10 Palestine: Central Council of the PLO meets in Ramalla and approves Chairman Arafat's proposal to nominate a Prime Minister—Abu Mazen.

19 Kuwait: American and British forces begin Gulf War 2 against Iraq. US Stealth bombers and Tomahawk Cruise Missiles strike leadership targets in and around Baghdad.

20 Iraq: US and British ground forces advance into southern Iraq, entering the port of Umm Qasr, near the city of Basra, while a second wave of air attacks hit Baghdad.

23 Iraq: Coalition forces seize airfields in western Iraq, and now control parts of Umm Qasr, Basra and Nasiriyah. Despite fierce resistance Coalition armoured units force a crossing of the Euphrates River at Nasiriyah and advance to within 100 miles of Baghdad. In the north the US launches a cruise missile attack on two extreme Islamic groups opposed to the

Patriotic Union of Kurdistan (PUK)—Kurds allied to the Coaltition. US forces then began airlifting troops into PUK controlled areas of northern Iraq, opening up a second front.

28 Kuwait: A Scud missile hits Kuwait City but inflicts only minor damage.

29 Iraq: Fierce fighting erupts at another vital bridge over the Euphrates in Samawah, but US forces smash through. The first suicide bombing on Coalition forces takes place, killing four American soldiers at Najaf.

30 Iraq: US forces fight and take Karbala, then Najaf, and Nasiriyah. Bombing raids continue on Baghdad and other Iraqi cities, and the Iraqis attempt to missile Kuwait. 600 British commandos attack near Basra, destroying Iraqi tanks and capturing nearly 300 prisoners.

April 2003
3 Iraq: US forces reach Saddam International Airport on the outskirts of Baghdad.

5 US armored forces enter Baghdad. Iraqi civilians begin widespread looting of the city.

7 Iraq: British forces reach the centre of Basra.

9 Iraq: Fall of Baghdad. Troops help Iraqi crowds topple the large statue of Saddam Hussein in the centre of Baghdad.

10 Iraq: Kurdish fighters take Kirkuk.

11 Iraq: US and Kurdish troops take Mosul.

13 Iraq: US forces enter Saddam's hometown of Tikrit.

15 Iraq: Tikrit falls and the Coalition declares the war to be effectively over.

June 2003
4 Fatah, Hamas and Islamic Jihad joined in killing four Israeli soldiers in Gaza despite the call to end violence from Fatah leaders.
Israel: Aqaba Summit—Abu Mazen and Ariel Sharon vow to stop violence and end Israeli occupation, following the protocols of the US inspired 'road map'. Hamas and Islamic Jihad also vow—to continue the violence.

10/11 Failed Israeli assassination attempt on Hamas leader Ahmed Rantissi (**10/6**) and Hamas suicide attack that kills 15 in Jerusalem (**11/6**) jeopardize the future of the road map.

August 2003
20 Israel: Hamas suicide bombing in a Jerusalem bus kills 21.

21 Israel: Israel declares all Hamas leaders targets and assassinates Ismail Abu Shanab. Others are also killed in widespread operations in the West bank.

September 2003
5 Israel: Failed Israeli assassination attempt on Hamas "spiritual leader" Ahmed Yassin,

20 Twin suicide bombings kill 15 in Israel.

October 2003
4 Israel: Palestinian Islam Jihad Suicide bomber kills 20 in Haifa.

5 Israel: Israeli airstrike a PLO training camp in Syria.